Kingdom C

Keys to the KINGDOM

A Guide to Entering the Kingdom Realm on Earth

Michael Gissibl

Copyright © 2018 Michael Gissibl
ISBN: 978-1-940359-62-5
Library of Congress Control Number: 2018933994
Published in the United States of America

All rights reserved as permitted under the U. S. Copyright Act of 1976. No part of this publication may be reproduced, distributed, or transmitted in any form or by any means, or stored in a database or retrieval system, without the expressed written permission of the author and publisher.

All scripture quotations, unless otherwise marked, are from THE HOLY BIBLE, NEW INTERNATIONAL VERSION®, NIV® Copyright © 1973, 1978, 1984, 2011 by Biblica, Inc.® Used by permission. All rights reserved worldwide.

Scripture quotations marked (HCSB®), are taken from the Holman Christian Standard Bible®, Copyright © 1999, 2000, 2002, 2003, 2009 by Holman Bible Publishers. Used by permission. HCSB® is a federally registered trademark of Holman Bible Publishers. All rights reserved.

Scripture quotations labeled (NASB) are taken from the New American Standard Bible®, Copyright © 1960, 1962, 1963, 1968, 1971, 1972, 1973, 1975, 1977, 1995 by The Lockman Foundation Used by permission. (www.Lockman.org). All rights reserved.

Scripture quotations labeled (NKJV) taken from the New King James Version®. Copyright © 1982 by Thomas Nelson, Inc. Used by permission. All rights reserved.

Scripture quotations marked (ESV) are taken from The ESV® Bible (The Holy Bible, English Standard Version®) copyright © 2001 by Crossway, a publishing ministry of Good News Publishers. ESV® Text Edition: 2011. The ESV® text has been reproduced in cooperation with and by permission of Good News Publishers. Unauthorized reproduction of this publication is prohibited. All rights reserved.

Cover Art by Jennifer Hunter Jones.
Connect with Jennifer's FaceBook page at "Glimpses of Glory Studio."
Her work can be purchased at www.glimpsesofglory.biz
or she can be contacted at jejones@integrity.com.

www.burkhartbooks.com
Bedford, Texas

Dedication & Acknowledgments

I dedicate this book to all the Overcomer's God is raising up. May this book become a catalyst for you to enter the Kingdom realm of consciousness. May this book become a tool in the Lord's hand that will prepare you to become a living stone—building material for Jesus to build His Church on earth from the Kingdom realm.

I want to thank my wife for granting me the freedom to be who I am. I also want to thank my spiritual father, Jack Taylor for allowing me to be who I am. When you have found friends that encourage you to be who you are, you have found a true friend. Sheila and Jack, thank you for encouraging me to be who I am. Thank you for being my friend!

Finally, thank you, Tim Taylor, for helping me publish this book. Thank you for empowering me when I had no strength. Thank you for your additions.

Contents

Dedication & Acknowledgments	
Preface	7
Introduction	9
Chapter 1 - Unity of the Faith	15
Chapter 2 - Kingdom Community	29
Chapter 3 - Experiencing Christ and His Kingdom —Enter the Kingdom Within	51
Chapter 4 - Four Principles for Experiencing Christ and His Kingdom Within	61
Chapter 5 - Walking in Resurrection Life through the Cross	79
Chapter 6 - From Warrior to Citizen	115
Chapter 7 - Love	129
Chapter - Third Rung Ladder Realm	139
Chapter 9 - Authority	155
Conclusion	163
About the Author	

Preface

The Kingdom Consciousness Series was birthed out of a ten day experience when I was taken into the Kingdom realm on earth in a more accelerated manner. During this time, I was living in a realm where the physical world and the Kingdom realm were unified in an experiential manner. The primary take aways from this time were twofold; 1) Keys needed to be appropriated in the coming years to begin ascension into the realm of the "come up here." This is the realm where Jesus abides and is awaiting the remnant whom He will use to build His Church; and 2) A preview of what to expect as we enter the Kingdom realm and discover the new identity realities that await us.

During a heightened and extended experience in the Kingdom realm of consciousness on earth, I was given much information for the coming years. There is a remnant of overcomers that are rising. They will need to be restored and sanctified for what the Lord is preparing for them. To rule and reign with Christ on planet earth, we must enter the mysteries of Heaven and begin putting into practice the keys of the Kingdom. We are discovering these keys and to those who are putting them into practice, transformation is taking place. A transformation that is transporting them into the realm of Kingdom consciousness. The realm of Jesus' invitation to *"Come up here."* This is the realm where the expressions and attributes of Jesus' Church are displayed and established on earth as it is in Heaven.

Introduction

"Bear with me a little, and I will show you that there are yet words to speak on God's behalf. I will fetch my knowledge from afar; I will ascribe righteousness to my Maker. For truly my words are not false; one who is perfect [whole] in knowledge is with you.

Job 36:2-4

For I long to see you so that I may impart some spiritual gift to you, that you may be established."

Romans 1:11 NASB

In Hebrews chapter 8 we discover a remarkable prophecy concerning the Lord and His people. This prophecy identifies a new way the Lord will relate to His people that is more closely aligned with Jesus' relationship with the Father while He walked the earth. A new covenant so profound in its effects that it will spark a restoration project in the heart of man that will change the systems ruling the earth. The emergence of the system responsible for holding the Kingdom realm of Consciousness is the fruit of this covenant. This system not only will change man's individual field of consciousness but awaken the collective consciousness of regional territory on the earth that's been given back to the Lord. The more people who have entered this covenant, the greater the expressions of this system and the more firmly rooted it will become. As we look into this prophecy, I pray the eyes of your understanding become enlightened to it. *"Behold I do a new thing, now it shall spring forth ..."* (Isaiah 43:19a).

"For this is the covenant that I will make with the house of Israel after those days, says the Lord: I will put My laws in their mind and write them on their hearts, and I will be their God, and they shall be My people. None of them shall teach his neighbor, and none his brother, saying, 'Know the Lord,' for all shall know Me, from the least of them to the greatest of them ... Now what is becoming obsolete and growing old is ready to vanish away."

Hebrews 8:10-13

The foundation of this covenant is the Lord "putting My laws in their mind." The Lord renews our minds by providing us with His information—information received while seeking first the Kingdom. This information contains content altogether different from information received outside of the Kingdom. Kingdom information is whole and brings consciousness of the "whole realm" we call the Kingdom realm of consciousness. Another name for this realm would be the Kingdom of Heaven on earth. Kingdom information contains laws limited to the Kingdom realm. "My laws" are more than a set of information, they are revelation of the laws that govern the Kingdom realm of consciousness.

Information not flowing from the Kingdom field is fragmented and forms consciousness of a realm outside that of the Kingdom realm. We call this realm the kingdom of darkness or the field of fragmented consciousness. All information flows from one of two sources—the tree of life (whole knowledge) or the tree of the knowledge of good and evil (fragmented information).

The importance of information and its role in forming consciousness cannot be overemphasized, for it is the essence of consciousness. The source of information determines which field of consciousness we find our existence. Information is assembled in our brains by neurons. The assembly of this information forms neuron systems. These systems pattern themselves with the outside world which brings the appearance of what is patterned in the brain through the information—by neurons. The assembly of this information forms neuron systems. Without the process of seeking first the information of the Kingdom, there can be no appropriation or realization of this covenant because only Kingdom information patterns the mind to reflect the Kingdom realm. The life of the covenant rests upon our carnal mind collapsing and the renewed mind emerging. We must endeavor to, above all, seek first the Kingdom. This discipline and this discipline alone is what provides the human mind with "My laws," the information responsible for growing the renewed mind. This is the information responsible for generating consciousness in the Kingdom system of rulership. Laws are a set of information that requires the essence of the information to be brought into existence and upheld. "My laws" are not merely a set of rules but specific information—information flowing from the Kingdom realm. This information is contained in an emerging field called Kingdomology and will be responsible for literally changing our minds. The change will be in the formation of the information received while seeking first the

Kingdom. This change will result in the growth of a new mind—the renewed mind—not change in the carnal mind because when the new comes, the old is done away with.

The results of living on earth with "My laws in their mind," according to Hebrews 8:11 is all of us shall "know the Lord." No one living in the covenant will need to teach anyone because all within the covenant will know the Lord. This is a remarkable promise. A promise that has come alive in this generation and is available to all who commit to Jesus' highest priority of seeking first the Kingdom. A covenant with such transformational power it will not only shift individuals perceptive capacities into another realm but will prove to be the catalyst for the transformation of the earth-changing the systems of rulership that govern its territory from that of darkness to light. I want to look more deeply into this covenant, specifically the process by which we come to know the Lord in this manner. I also want to bring to light the new and improved way in which we will "know" the Lord. It's my intent to uncover a Kingdom key to accessing the Lord and His Kingdom to the measure in which this covenant promises.

What did the Lord mean when He said, *"None of them shall teach his neighbor, and none his brother, saying, 'Know the Lord,' for all shall know Me, from the least of them to the greatest of them."* What could possibly bring about such a transformation in a covenant people that would yield a cessation of the need to teach each other? Allow me to explain. The phrase, *"Know the Lord, for all shall know me"* can be understood by first looking closely at the two words "know." When we understand the meaning and context of these two words, the covenant opens to us, and we receive a greater understanding. As the eyes of our understanding become enlightened, it becomes necessary for us to step into the revelation, marinating in it until we see the content emerging.

The first word "know" can be defined "to know by experience." There are two ways in which we come to know something by experience. The first is pursuing the thing we desire to experience. The second is to condition our minds in the field of study that opens what we aspire to experience. I say this to point out an important distinction. Those entering this covenant need to pursue the information path of knowing by experience, not the pursuing of the desired attribute. The ladder seems easier, but God would not have established the foundation of this covenant to be putting His information in our minds if He didn't need us to seek the field of information. *"Putting My laws in their minds"* implies a process of receiving Kingdom information. Be it as it may, let us continue. The second word "know" can be defined "a gateway to access the Kingdom realm from a physical plane." With this foundational understanding, let's revisit the covenant. The Lord is essentially saying the following; "I am going to place a group into a covenant with Me. This covenant will hinge upon the renewed mind that I will grow in them as I release *"My laws into their mind."* The renewed mind is My gateway through which to experience Me and My Kingdom realm, from a physical plane. The renewed mind is the vehicle which transports you into My Kingdom realm—a realm that is resting on the physical plane of earth. The effects will have such an impact on you that you will not need to teach anyone living in this covenant because, in part, the spirit of Wisdom and Revelation will be fully opened to you. Rather, all your attention relating to teaching will be devoted to instructing those outside My covenant. There will come a point in this process that the renewed mind will become the predominant field of vision in which My covenant people will see. In this realm, you will have developed an ongoing and growing success of 'only doing what you see the Father doing.'"

Author's Note: As we embark on seeking first the Kingdom with the intent of allowing the information of God to renew our minds, we must guard against pride and arrogance. Entering the Kingdom realm necessitates great humility and brokenness. Regular check-ups are needed in order to make sure you are not becoming prideful. We know Satan fell like lighting but what we must keep in mind is that we too can fall just as hard and fast. Pride comes before a fall, and in the Kingdom realm, our flesh surely will be tempted to become prideful. Remember the beatitudes and know that pain and opposition are tools used to keep you in the Kingdom realm of consciousness.

> *"Now when all the people were baptized, Jesus was also baptized, and while He was praying, heaven was opened."*
>
> Luke 3:21

This passage records that "heaven was opened" while Jesus was being baptized in water. John's water baptism signified the immersion into the study of the message of the Kingdom—the information responsible for growing the renewed mind. The result? Heaven was opened! Keep in mind; John was a teacher of the message of the Kingdom. He was the forerunner that carried the message of the Kingdom, calling for the same change of mind as Jesus. Whenever anyone wanted to be baptized by John, they were making a public statement; "I'm committing to immersing myself in the teaching of the one baptizing." By allowing John to baptize Him, Jesus was publicly confirming what He had been doing privately—seeking the information of the Kingdom. Taking this a step further, Jesus' statement: *"I only do what I see My Father doing,"* implies that He received a consistent flow of information from the Kingdom realm. John the Baptist, when he declared, *"I baptize with water ... "* was identifying his ministry as a teacher of the message of the Kingdom. Those that were baptized by John were identifying with his ministry and teaching. To enter the Kingdom we all must be baptized by water and the Spirit.

John declared "repent," change your mind, because the Kingdom is here. You can rest assured that heaven will open as you immerse yourself in the information of the Kingdom. To seek first the Kingdom is to become baptized in the information of the Kingdom. As you are brought up out of this information, heaven is opened, and your entrance into the Kingdom realm on earth begins. You leave the place of confinement in one realm and emerge out from that place, breathing in new life.

> *"He then added, 'Very truly I tell you, you will see heaven open, and the angels of God ascending and descending on' the Son of Man.'"*
> John 1:51 NIV

Jesus, in John chapter One, was addressing Nathaniel's faith when He declared, *"Do you believe just because I told you I saw you under the fig tree? You will see greater things than these."* In other words, He was telling Nathaniel that he had faith, but as he continued to walk with Jesus, Jesus would change his mind to the point where "'he will see greater things" than merely an attribute of His Kingdom—a word of knowledge. Nathaniel, would see the Kingdom. He would enter a covenant with Jesus, actualized as his mind was renewed, that would enable him to enter a gateway into His Kingdom realm on earth. *"Very truly I tell you, you will see heaven open ..."* (John 1:51)

> *"After these things I looked, and behold, a door standing open in heaven, and the first voice which I had heard ... said, 'Come up here, and I will show you what must take place after these things.'"*
> Revelation 4:1

There is a door standing open. A gateway into a covenant where access into the Kingdom realm on earth is available to all who choose to receive the information of the Kingdom taken in while seeking first the Kingdom. Multitudes are rising with a firm commitment to seek first the Kingdom. I pray this book become a springboard for you to enter into such a discipline. Committing to it until you enter the gateway which leads into the Kingdom realm of consciousness.

Volume Two of the *Kingdom Consciousness Series, The Keys to the Kingdom*, is a continuation of Volume One, *Kingdom Consciousness: A Generation's Call to Come Up Here*. It's my prayer that this book imparts to you the spiritual gift of entering the process in which you are lead into this realm. I long to see the eyes of your understanding enlightened in the knowledge of God so that the riches of your inheritance would be realized. I long to see the eyes of your understanding enlightened so that the Lord may find another living stone in which to build His Kingdom Church on earth, from the realm of Kingdom consciousness.

CHAPTER 1

Unity of the Faith

"I appeal to you, brothers and sisters, in the name of our Lord Jesus Christ, that all of you agree with one another in what you say and that there be no divisions among you, but that you be perfectly united in mind and thought."

1 Corinthians 1:10

Building in the Kingdom Realm of Consciousness

To break ground is to dig into the earth at the start of a construction project. The purpose is to build something that will serve the culture and community of the territory in which the building is erected. We have one earth but two systems resting upon the earth. Jesus only builds in the Kingdom realm—His system of light. Unless He finds "living stones" in His Kingdom realm, He has no building material in which to continue construction. The church built by man is constructed with material from the carnal realm of consciousness. It is the church we are most familiar with (the church we are conditioned in and perceive reality from) which has been built in the system of darkness. Jesus' Church is built with material found in His Kingdom realm of consciousness. Jesus' building material, living stones, must first ascend into the Kingdom realm before He will continue building His Church. Jesus has worked with man's church to grow some fruit, but only Jesus' Church, the Church He's building in the Kingdom realm of consciousness, grows lasting fruit.

For over 1900 years, the Lord's influence has been limited on earth due to His need to enter the carnal realm and visit man's church in the system of darkness. The book of Daniel calls this system the kingdom of man. The dawning of a new day has arrived. Jesus is once again finding living stones on the earth that have entered His realm, the realm of

Kingdom consciousness. Through repentance, a change of mind from the substance of the carnal to the substance of the renewed, these students of the Kingdom have left the carnal realm of the kingdom of man and have ascended into Christ's Kingdom realm of consciousness. This transformation by way of transportation through the renewing of the mind has given Jesus legal access to once again continue construction of His Church on earth—the Church that expressed itself briefly during the book of Acts era. This is the Church that was living in "unity of mind." The living stones were assembled on local territory to the point that the spirit and power of Elijah dominated the physical territory in which they occupied, introducing the multitudes to another realm of existence. This Kingdom realm of consciousness manifested the culture and social norms of Heaven on earth. It is an atmosphere that opens another field of consciousness and provides those inhabiting the territory with a new way of life.

Since the days Jesus walked the earth, He has extended an invitation to participate in His building project. This building project is taking place, not in the kingdom of man—the carnal realm of consciousness resting upon the earth—but in His system of rulership—the Kingdom realm of consciousness simultaneously resting upon the earth. The first century disciples, by accepting the identity of a student and committing to seek first the Kingdom, became the group Jesus took into His realm of consciousness on earth. These disciples grew to be the foundation of living stones. These living stones entered the system where the mysteries of the Kingdom were opened and construction of His Church on earth began. These disciples became the first to accept the invitation to co-labor with Christ in His realm to build His Church. Jesus broke ground on the day of Pentecost but not to many decades later the building project halted. The construction material ran out as the discipline of seeking first the Kingdom was lost—the vehicle of transportation into the Kingdom realm was abandoned. The living stones, the students of Jesus, became ineffective in passing down the discipline of seeking first the Kingdom and thus lost the forward motion of colonizing the earth from the Kingdom realm. Since the rediscovery of the discipline of seeking first the Kingdom, Jesus has resumed construction in an accelerated manner and is gathering living stones with which to build. Those that enter the Kingdom realm of consciousness through the narrow gate of seeking first the Kingdom are those who become building materials in the hand of the Lord. To enter the Kingdom experientially you must become a disciple of Jesus and cultivate the discipline of seeking first the Kingdom. This discipline renews the mind and is Jesus' prescribed means of entering His system of rulership on earth. The primary purpose for entering the Kingdom realm of consciousness is to provide Jesus with living stones in which to build expressions of the Kingdom through His Church on the earth. Jesus is longing to bring into existence the highest expression of the "unity of mind"—the commanded blessing of Kingdom consciousness once again made visible on earth.

> *"Behold, how good and how pleasant it is for brethren to dwell together in unity! For there the Lord commanded the blessing—Life forevermore."*
>
> Psalm 133:1 & 3a NKJV

Collective Kingdom consciousness is manifested through the "unity of mind" spoken of in Acts and will be shown to be responsible for the transformation of cities. There are currently several dormant principles in Acts 19 that will be resurrected in the coming years. Out of these resurrected principles will emerge small groups sprouting the "unity of mind" grown in the field of Kingdom consciousness. These groups will become models that will be used to transform the collective consciousness of their specific regions, displaying the culture of Heaven to inhabitants of the land. These regions will not only become refugee camps but will prove to be the conduits through which the Kingdom Nation on earth is established and expressed as the primary system of rulership. The Kingdom of Heaven is a country whose rule and reign is presently upon the earth. Until we enter the realm of Kingdom consciousness, we are veiled to the experience and influence of this truth. Heaven awaits the rise of the Overcomers. The ones who will enter the realm of Kingdom consciousness, discover the country of Heaven on earth, and begin ruling and reigning with Christ. These Mighty Ones will rise with the leaves on their renewed minds that will be for the healing of the nations! If not you then who? If not now, then when?

In order for Jesus to begin expressing His Kingdom on earth, the Church must enter the "unity of faith" found in the realm of Kingdom consciousness. This unity will be realized as groups of disciples enter the sheep pen of seeking first the Kingdom. Seeking first the Kingdom will provide us with the substance responsible for growing and developing the renewed mind. Those committed to abiding in this discipline will become the overcomers of the carnal mind and will not only discover the non-dual nature of the realm of the Kingdom and the physical realm, but will become the workers sent to bring in the harvest (see Luke 10:2). These will be those entrusted to spread not only the message of the gospel of the Kingdom but influence the earth with the culture of Heaven— Jesus' way. These workers are being equipped to express great signs and wonders, the tools used to harvest the souls awaiting their entrance into the Kingdom. There are groups presently being assembled who, through their study of the field of Kingdomology, will become models for the Kingdoms expression. The more devotion to their study in the field of Kingdomology, the greater the unity of faith. The greater the unity of faith, the more influential the group will become.

Like any field of study, in order to gain traction in culture there needs to be a group willing to pioneer the field. Once the groundwork is laid and the foundation established, the field becomes available to introduce into culture. Every field of study has gone through this model before it permeated a culture's consciousness and became part of the landscape of law in society. The Kingdom is no different. In order to enter the field of consciousness in which the field of study carries, you must become willing to dedicate your life to the field of study long enough that the information renews your mind to form new conscious awareness— awareness in the field you are studying. Like a school of psychology, Jesus took a group of individuals and made them students of the Kingdom. He initiated the field of Kingdomology and crowned His students with entrance into His domain—the field of Kingdom consciousness. He did this by changing their minds with the information of the Kingdom. This cause-effect action of receiving information of the Kingdom and entering the field of Kingdom consciousness is a key to experiencing unity of faith which is also called unity of mind. Two or more people carrying the same belief system constitutes a unity of faith. The belief system becomes the patterns of the mind that constitute unity of mind. A secret of the Kingdom is that unity of mind holds collective consciousness of the Kingdom which will be used to express and uphold Kingdom culture on earth. The disciples became the prototype for the generation that will be conferred with the practice of ruling regional territory with Christ the King. It's essential that we have solid understanding of our position in this matter. That position being co-laborers with Christ, allowing Him to rule through us while we effortlessly rest in our seat in Heaven. Such will be the state of all who submit as students of the message of the Kingdom, allowing the information of the Kingdom to transform us into overcomers. The overcomers who overcome self-life, empowering Christ in us to become the influence on earth.

These students are emerging as the pioneers of Jesus' Church and have began spreading a field of study, the field of Kingdomology with the mandate to make students out of nations (see Matthew 28:19). Those that committed to seeking first the Kingdom entered the field of consciousness of the Kingdom and discovered a new way of living in the realm of the Kingdom. A disciple of Jesus discovers the Kingdom the same way a psychologist discovers the hidden truths residing in the soul—by studying the field to the degree that the realm of consciousness contained in psychology is opened to them. Once that realm of consciousness appears, a new world emerges that presents the discoverer with territory yet to be explored. The pioneers of psychology became so effective in presenting and spreading their discovered field that today, several billion humans are directly affected by it. The discovery of the Kingdom field of consciousness begins when you commit to walking in the field where the Kingdom lays—the field of Kingdomology.

There are realms in the Kingdom much like there are cities in a state. Each one has its own characteristics and serves specific purposes resulting in the sprouting and growing of the Kingdom seeds within. It is possible that Saints on earth only access a part of the Kingdom whose function is to prepare for colonization of earth. It's impossible for you to experience the whole Kingdom. We will be spending eternity delighting ourselves in the ever-increasing expanse of His marvelous rule. We will make a distinction between the Kingdom to come and the eternal Kingdom. It appears the Kingdom realms are in relative proximity to the King as the deeper levels require deeper practical purity. This section lays out principles for entering higher levels in the Kingdom which is coming. Keep in mind, we don't move about in the Kingdom apart from the "carrying to and fro" by the Holy Spirit or His assigned agents. This is His Kingdom. He is King. Our lives are not our own! We have the indescribable privilege of standing in His presence waiting to be of service. We must enter the discipline of disconnecting from our Wills, nailing it to the cross daily.

During my ten day experience in a deeper state of Kingdom consciousness, I was walking in a realm I had yet to experience. The measure of the Kingdom realm of consciousness that I had, to that point been living in was suddenly expanded. The Kingdom's appearance was more defined and available as my spiritual senses became alive in a heightened way. My Kingdom community grew as I realized there is more to Jesus' Church than humans living on the earth. The presence of the Lord was on me like a wool blanket, but the essence of His presence took on added substance not experienced previously. I had an awareness of the Kingdom realm like never before as my field of consciousness became enveloped in the non-duel nature of the spiritual and physical realm anew. I saw heavenly beings in my midst, and the awareness of Christ's presence was like nothing I'd experienced outside of momentary supernatural experiences. I was consumed, overtaken by the Kingdom in a fuller measure. The impurity and filth of television and other activity in the carnal realm became more evident to me. All I wanted to do was remain still and in awe of the Kingdom's wonder.

I'm convinced, the more we understand the ways of the Lord and the more we are committed to obedience to His ways, the higher Kingdom dimensions we will enter. Those with clean hands and a pure heart will ascend the hill of the Lord. Judging from an experience I had in 2013 of the temple being restored, I believe we will be abiding in some of these higher Kingdom dimensions in the coming years—dimensions Ezekiel, Isaiah, and our beloved Savior walked in. I'm hesitant to use the term "higher" because it's more like "normal" in the Kingdom, but there is validity in describing these levels as "higher" or "deeper."

Working with Holy Spirit to cleanse the temple is essential to functioning from the Kingdom realm of consciousness. The most pressing need of cleansing is the mind. To be transported into the Kingdom realm we must renew our minds with Kingdom information. We do this by committing to seek first the information of the Kingdom until the realm of Kingdom consciousness appears in our subjective experience. Once our primary field of consciousness is that of the Kingdom realm, then we come under the control of the domain of the King on a new level and begin preparation for the transformation of cities and nations. Each time the eyes of your understanding become enlightened, know that your mind is being renewed with the information responsible for ushering you into the Kingdom realm of consciousness.

> *"Not everyone who says to me, 'Lord, Lord,' will enter the Kingdom of Heaven, but only the one who does the will of my Father who is in Heaven. Many will say to me on that day, 'Lord, Lord, did we not prophesy in your name and your name drive out demons and in your name perform many miracles?' Then I will tell them plainly, 'I never knew you. Away from me, you evildoers!"*
>
> Matthew 7:21-23

I believe this statement has application for both the Kingdom coming on earth and the eternal Kingdom. When Jesus said "away from me you evildoer" He was saying "take a step back, for the place you are standing is reserved for someone more intimately acquainted with me." Judging from my experiences, it appears that closeness of proximity with Christ is directly related to choices we make moving forward. The degree to which we cleanse our minds and body with Holy Spirit's empowerment determines where we stand before the Lord. This has practical application since nothing unholy can stand in His presence. The closer we get, the cleaner we need to be (Look at the priests in the Old Testament. Didn't they have to perform ceremonial cleansing before entering the Holy of Holies?).

The key to moving closer to Christ in His Kingdom is doing the will of the Father in Heaven. The following are three principles for preparing yourself to step into this most desired of pursuits.

God opposes the proud but gives grace to the humble. Fasting is the Kingdom means of humbling yourself. The pinnacle of fasting moves beyond food and encompasses starving yourself of all activity outside the pursuit of Christ and His Kingdom, particularly seeking the Kingdom first. By looking closely at your day, you will likely find it's filled with things of this world—TV, entertainment, carnal communication, your thought life, earthly desires, etc. Taking inventory provides you clear vision as to where you stand. The purer your decisions are— second by second, minute by minute, and hour by hour— the greater the potential flow of Kingdom consciousness. You see what you seek. Information carries its essence and manifests itself to all who give themselves over to it. Kingdom information is no different.

Michael Gissibl

"Therefore, since we are surrounded by such a great cloud of witnesses, let us throw off everything that hinders and the sin that so easily entangles. And let us run with perseverance the race marked out for us."
Hebrews 12:1

To be entertained is to enter containment. Entering containment is only negative when the containment is outside the Kingdom. To be entertained by seeking first the Kingdom places you in containment of the Kingdom. God's entertainment is the only form of entertainment that not only satisfies the deepest recesses of the soul but contains substance responsible for transporting our consciousness from this world into His. The inhabitants of the earth have been entangled in activity that has captured and imprisoned us in the realm of the carnal mind's consciousness. Throwing off this entanglement frees us from the hindrance's that keep us from entering containment in the Kingdom realm of consciousness.

The most important activity to speeding up God's transforming process is seeking first the Kingdom. Continually providing your brain with information on the Kingdom is the key to being transformed by the renewing of your mind. It is essential you guard against strife in your pursuit of transformation. Although we have a responsibility, it is always God who works in us both to do and to Will for His good pleasure. No man can truthfully take any credit in the Kingdom. You may decide to seek information of the Kingdom, but it's the form within the information that brings about the change. We truly are at the mercy of God and in need of His Divine empowerment. Furthermore, the posture in the Kingdom is that of resting and receiving. You must remain seated in the Kingdom realm of consciousness, for to be in any other position is to fall like lightning.

Genesis tells us:

"Enoch lived sixty-five years and begot Methuselah. After he begot Methuselah, Enoch walked with God three hundred years and had sons and daughters. So all the days of Enoch were three hundred and sixty-five years. And Enoch walked with God; and he was not, for God took him."
Genesis 5:21-24 NKJV

We are living in the days of Enoch, the days of being taken in and abiding in Heaven. A key to entrance is leaving our past. Doing so puts off the old nature, a prerequisite to abiding in Heaven. As it was said of Enoch, *"and he was not,"* so too are the days we are living. These "was nots" are rising into the realm of the Kingdom. In the same way, Enoch gave birth to the longest living human, so too are the "sons of Enoch" giving birth to the longest living Kingdom, the eternal reign of Christ and His Kingdom.

The timeline of Kingdom wakefulness and the collapse of the present rule of darkness is patiently resting in the renewed minds of Kingdom Saints. The earth has been given to all who enter the Kingdom through the renewed mind.

> *"The highest heavens are the Lord's, but the earth he has given to the sons of man."*
>
> Psalm 115:16

It is incumbent as a charged duty and responsibility for us to make nations our classrooms and their people our students—students of THIS gospel of the Kingdom. The result will be the Saints bringing awareness of and progressive wakefulness towards Heaven on earth. The collective collapse of darkness on earth is contingent upon the collapse of its existence within the individual Saint before the systems of rulership on earth topple. It's a good thing God's ways are not ours; otherwise, darkness would rule the earth forever.

Let me make a distinction between two "Holinesses." When you were born again, you were clothed in the righteousness of Christ. He exchanged your sin for His righteousness, thereby making you Holy and righteous. You have been made the righteousness of God in Christ not because of what you do, but because of what He's done. This is an eternal righteousness that has placed you in right standing with the King—forever accepted and welcomed. There also is a holiness on earth that permeates the human side of you. This holiness must be realized and established in the body and soul in order to ascend the hill of the Lord. In a practical way, living in the Kingdom places you in another facet of the King's presence. This facet is the practical holiness of the Lord. The higher Kingdom realms you enter, the closer you will be to the Holy One. This necessitates a purity in the human body, for no flesh can stand in this presence.

During my ten day experience of walking in "higher Kingdom dimensions," I felt the weight of God's holiness having effect on my physical body. I knew I needed to sanctify myself at a deeper level. I removed earthly, carnal stimuli, reduced my calorie intake, made a conscious effort to keep things originating from the carnal realm out of my ear and eye gates, and focused on pure thinking while reducing sleep slightly (the desert fathers taught too much sleep brought spiritual lethargy). I made a conscious effort to remove as much carnality from entering my soul gates while *"striking a blow to my body and making it a slave to my spirit man"* (1Corinthians 9:27). This brought my Kingdom awareness to a higher level.

Author's Note: It is also noteworthy to mention that I struggled with a "galloping" heart after leaving the Lord's Will while the spirit of Revelation was escorting me in the Kingdom realm. In one instance, while in a specific place in the Kingdom, having been taken into the future, I disengaged from the moment and chose to move further into the future. This decision was a selfish engagement of my Will that had consequences. I was sternly rebuked by the Lord and drew back into the place I had been. This experience opened my eyes to many principles relating to living in the Kingdom realm of consciousness on earth. Perhaps the most sobering is knowing we still possess a free will, even in the Kingdom realm, and are capable of choosing fleshly desires. I believe what caused my heart to beat unnaturally for almost two weeks was a moment of acting on a fleshly desire in the Kingdom presence of the Lord. I believe the story of Ananias and Sapphira are Biblical examples of a similar bodily response; only their encounter ended in death. I do not believe they were killed by the Lord; rather they entered an environment where the presence of the Lord was of a different nature. This environment is the Kingdom realm of consciousness in operation on the earth through the unity of mind of the Church Jesus is building. The earthly Church has been so conditioned by the Lord's presence in the carnal realm that we think we know Him. We think His presence is limited to goosebumps, loving caresses, an emotional experience, and an occasional supernatural expression. This is true in a sense because we have yet to meet the Living God in His dwelling place. I did. Ananias and Sapphira did too, and because we were not pure in heart, we suffered. I am not saying this to scare you or to be a Debbie Downer. I am simply bringing to light an important fact of Kingdom living. To abide in the Kingdom on earth, we must carry our crosses daily and be ready to cut away all flesh as the Spirit leads. The first century Church was birthed in the Kingdom realm, not the carnal realm. The first century Church loved

Jesus primarily through obedience to His command to seek first the Kingdom. This act of obedience moved them into the realm of the "come up here," the place where Jesus builds His Church. We are once again approaching the dawning of Churches being taken into the realm of the "come up here." As we enter this realm of existence, we must prepare to encounter added character traits of the King of kings and Lord of lords. His holiness is one of those character traits the earthly Church has little experience with.

In the same way, humans require oxygen, so too do "Kingdom dwellers" require practical Holiness. Although Jesus has in a real sense taken our sins and given us His righteousness, we nevertheless need clean hands and a pure heart. When John experienced a deeper realm of Heaven on earth, his body was unable to stand upright.

> *"In His right hand He held seven stars, and out of His mouth came a sharp two-edged sword; and His face was like the sun shining in its strength. When I saw Him, I fell at His feet like a dead man. And He placed His right hand on me."*
>
> Revelation 1:16

Jesus may have been placing his hand on John to bring a deeper level of cleansing to his body, empowering him to get up and continue. Keep in mind that John was on earth when He was experiencing the resurrected Christ—on earth in the realm of the Kingdom.

A Word Picture of Life in the Kingdom Realm on Earth

> *"Now an angel of the Lord said to Philip, 'Rise and go toward the south to the road that goes down from Jerusalem to Gaza.' This is a desert place. And he rose and went. And there was an Ethiopian, a eunuch, a court official of Candace, queen of the Ethiopians, who was in charge of all her treasure. He had come to Jerusalem to worship and was returning, seated in his chariot, and he was reading the prophet Isaiah. And the Spirit said to Philip, 'Go over and join this chariot.' So Philip ran to him and heard him reading Isaiah the prophet and asked, 'Do you understand what you are reading?' And he said, 'How can I, unless someone guides me?' And he invited Philip to come up and*

sit with him. Now the passage of Scripture that he was reading was this: Like a sheep he was led to the slaughter and like a lamb before its shearer is silent, so he opens not his mouth. In his humiliation justice was denied him. Who can describe his generation for his life is taken away from the earth. And the eunuch said to Philip, about whom, I ask you, does the prophet say this, about himself or about someone else? Then Philip opened his mouth, and beginning with this Scripture he told him the good news about Jesus. And as they were going along the road they came to some water, and the eunuch said, 'See, here is water! What prevents me from being baptized?' And he commanded the chariot to stop, and they both went down into the water, Philip, and the eunuch, and he baptized him. And when they came up out of the water, the Spirit of the Lord carried Philip away, and the eunuch saw him no more and went on his way rejoicing. But Philip found himself at Azotus, and as he passed through he preached the gospel to all the towns until he came to Caesarea."

Acts 8:26-40

A picture of activity flowing from life in the Kingdom on earth is found in the above passage. Although this story is a natural expression, its representation sheds light on what I saw and experienced during my time in the Kingdom realm, particularly in relation to how we live and move, or rather are moved in the Kingdom on earth. Here we see Phillip connected with Heaven as he receives orders from an angel and, in obedience, expresses the commands on earth, bringing to pass, in a moment of time, an expression of the Lord's Prayer *"on earth as it is in Heaven."* When he completes his task, Phillip is transported and continues Kingdom activity elsewhere. Notice his existence began in Heaven but expressed the plans of Heaven on earth, effectively colonizing a territory of earth with Heaven. As you find yourself in Heaven, firmly rooted in union and fellowship with Christ, which in practical terms takes place in your spirit, anticipate Him transporting you from place to place, giving assignments to legislate on earth. There seems to be a "posture" in the Kingdom which goes something like this: you spend your day, moment by moment, before the Lord, consciously aware of His presence. This is "happening" in your spirit which is one with the Holy Spirit. Until you learn to live out of your spirit, it becomes important to discipline yourself to "check in" with your spirit as often as you remember. At the same time your awareness is conditioned in the life of the spirit, your Will is engaged towards anticipating "a call" to do His bidding. Your spiritual eyes and ears are fixed on Christ in you, intently and patiently awaiting a directive from His throne. As you wait, you are provided the indescribable privilege of fellowshipping with the Living God, enjoying a peace that surpasses all understanding. As He sees fit, He transports you to different places within His Kingdom to receive a commission. You're then assigned to bring into the earth realm substance received in Heaven. The release of such substance not only expresses an attribute of Heaven, but establishes the essence of Heaven on earth. As a community of THE WAY begins walking in daily expressions of Heaven, the culture and ways of the Kingdom begins forming. Once the culture of Heaven comes alive, the Lord has His model to then present to other communities, cities and ultimately nations—if the community holds fast without wavering. The nations will not become the Church's inheritance until this model of Kingdom cultural growth is implemented.

The model for Kingdom cultural growth could be summed up as follows:

1. Seek first the Kingdom and His righteousness

2. Receiving the information of the Kingdom forms the basis for the unity of faith—the unity of the belief system of Christ and His Kingdom, the renewed mind.

3. When individuals seeking first the Kingdom come together, varying measured amounts of unity of faith, which is grown as we seek first the Kingdom, forms the unity of mind which brings the outward appearance of the Kingdom onto the earth.

In other words, seeking first the Kingdom awakens inward expressions of the Kingdom to the eyes of our understanding. As we come together with other like-minded individuals seeking the Kingdom, the assembled unity of mind makes room for the outward expressions of the Kingdoms culture on earth.

Life in the Kingdom consists of abiding in the presence of the King experientially, practically, and literally. In doing so, you make yourself available to be used as a vessel in fulfilling His Will on earth. Kingdom citizens are like angels going in and coming out from the presence of the Lord—like a line of taxis waiting outside a resort. The moment the attendant raises his hand for service, you move towards his desired end of fulfilling the command. When the assignment is complete, you go back to headquarters where you await your next assignment. What's astonishingly beautiful is how the King personally escorts you during the mission—not only supporting and cheering you on but infusing you with His power and authority to successfully enact His desires.

Jesus, in Matthew 6, made two distinctions by defining life as either the pursuit of things or seeking first the Kingdom. In perhaps a more real sense than we could have imagined, there is "life" found when seeking first the Kingdom. The two life sources generate not only two very different conscious experiences but move you into very specific fields of consciousness. One field is of the Kingdom and presents to you the "at present" existence of it on earth. The other life source stems from a system of rulership begun by Satan way back in the garden. This system is known as the kingdom of ignorance-darkness. One is eternal and the other temporal. One is formed while receiving information of the whole while the other is generated from the information of the parts. Eating from the tree of the knowledge of good and evil ensures conscious experience of Satan's system of rulership. Its fruit is fragmented information which assembles the carnal mind which is consciousness in the kingdom of ignorance. Eating from the tree of life opens conscious experience of the whole which is the Kingdom. The fruit grown on the tree of life is information of the whole which assembles the renewed mind—consciousness in Christ's Kingdom.

This way of life in the Kingdom was further validated to me one morning as I was in the spirit and taken into a room where I was given a parable. I was shown two houses. One was a government home. Within this home, a family was living which made the dwelling place not only a government home but a family home. The Lord began sharing a facet of how the Kingdom works. I saw how He transported His royal family members around similar to how He transported Phillip. We are living in the days of great change. Perhaps the most influential change will accelerate once the Church leaves its earthly identity in the carnal realm and steps into its heavenly abode. Repentance begins this process, seeking first the Kingdom transports us into our heavenly abode of consciousness in the Kingdom.

CHAPTER 2

Kingdom Community

Kingdom community must be built upon the foundation of the unity of faith that grows and develops the unity of mind. This unity of faith emerges as groups of people seek first the information of the Kingdom—the substance responsible for growing unity of mind. Kingdom community God's way cannot be realized nor expressed any other way. All other attributes of Kingdom community sprout from the unity of mind which is planted in the soil of seeking first the Kingdom. As we stay true to the above mentioned principles, and enter into there disciplines, the realm of Kingdom consciousness is opened to us and we begin seeing added characteristics of community given to us by the Lord. Even those attributes that no eye has seen or mind has conceived.

Kingdom community is comprised of more than the Saints living in the Kingdom realm on earth. Kingdom community includes any heavenly being the Lord chooses to bring into your field of consciousness. All for the purpose of building up the Church, never for the gratification of the flesh. Jesus is Lord in this realm and chooses when, where, and how to engage His heavenly host. It's important for us to prepare for such an addition to the Church Jesus is building. To make room for heavenly host in our midst is an important step in the process of becoming mature. To reach the measure of the stature of the fullness of Christ we need all that God has for us.

I am not implying that we seek after this heavenly host. In fact, I am vehemently opposing such a thing. We are to seek first the Kingdom of God, His righteousness and seek only to do what we see the Father doing. No time or energy is to be devoted to seeking the heavenly host. To do so would be idolatry at the least. In the Kingdom realm of consciousness, if we are to look for anyone or anything, let us look to Jesus, the author, and finisher of our faith.

The Saints of the past are nearby all who enter the Kingdom on earth. They have a role to play in the lives of the overcomers. While we don't want to give much attention to this, we do however need to acknowledge this and understand that Jesus has incorporated our brothers and sisters who have gone before us.

> *"Therefore, since we are surrounded by such a great cloud of witnesses, let us throw off everything that hinders and the sin that so easily entangles. And let us run with perseverance the race marked out for us."*
> Hebrews 12:1

The Seattle Seahawks are an NFL football team. At any given time, a team has 11 players on the field, unified in their goal. However, Seattle claims to have what they call a 12th man. That being the "cloud of witnesses" they are surrounded by—their fans. By acknowledging their fan base and simply receiving their cheers, the Seahawks claim something is added to those "running the race" that would otherwise not be received. The cheering of their fans, in a literal sense, adds to their outcome, making them something they were not, previous to receiving what the "cloud of witnesses" had to offer. Both the Seattle Seahawks and their opponents bear witness to this reality.

In the following chapter, the author of Hebrew's introduces another being invited into the lives of the Saints who walk in the Kingdom on earth.

> *"Do not forget to show hospitality to strangers, for by so doing some people have shown hospitality to angels without knowing it."*
> Hebrews 13:1

Throughout the life of the disciples, there was regular interaction with angels. They received direction, key bits of information and comfort from the heavenly host. Not to mention the impartation of the divine nature they must have received just being in their presence. Why? Because they were part of the Church Jesus was building—the Church being built in the realm of the Kingdom. I cannot emphasize enough the importance of not pursuing the heavenly host—not even the slightest. My intent in introducing these heavenly beings is to enlighten you to an important part of the Kingdom Church in the coming years. The Kingdom community on earth is made up of more than humans, Jesus and the Holy Spirit. The Kingdom on earth is an extension of the eternal Kingdom of Heaven. As you are led into deeper measures of Kingdom consciousness, do not be surprised as you encounter those occupying this eternal realm on earth. Let their presence be a reminder that you are equipped to a greater degree than you previously thought. Receive from them in their presence, always remembering your task—to seek the Kingdom, His righteousness and to only do what you see the Father doing.

We are embarking on a journey that is leading *"to the city with foundations, whose architect and builder is God"* (Hebrews 11:10). The inhabitants of this city have been its foundation, waiting for us, the building material of God. They settled here long before us. We need to honor and esteem those that went before us, accepting them as foundations the Lord will build upon. Accept that you are the building material, the living stones that need to rest upon this foundation. The following is a rendering of what I saw and heard during a moment in the Kingdom realm of consciousness. The following is also an introduction of two members of Jesus' Kingdom Church, eagerly awaiting their freedom to begin appearing to us in the manner in which the Lord intended. Don't look for them outside of yourself, for the Kingdom always appears first within. Rather, seek first the Kingdom and sooner or later they will appear. I pray this key become a catalyst for you to, not seek the heavenly host but seek first the Kingdom. I will do my best to articulate a mystery of the Kingdom, hidden for such a time as this.

The Spirit of Wisdom and the Spirit of Revelation Added to Kingdom Community

I was taken in the spirit and found myself sitting in a boat. Suddenly the Lord spoke, "Launch out into the deep, and let down your nets for a catch."

"That the God of our Lord Jesus Christ, the Father of glory, may give unto you the spirit of wisdom and revelation in the knowledge of him" (Ephesians 1:7). It is the Lord's highest desire to give you the spirit of wisdom and revelation. Notice, His desire is not to give you a revelation or a measure of wisdom but rather the spirits themselves. Two heavenly hosts dwelling in the Kingdom realm. The living, abiding presence of the spirit of wisdom and the spirit of revelation is the expressed goal of Paul's prayer here. We have settled for a revelation when the Lord's heart is to awaken us to the abiding nature of the spirit of revelation. We have settled for the pursuit of wisdom when the Lord wants to entrust us with the abiding presence of the spirit of wisdom. Imagine with me for a moment that the spirit of revelation is abiding in you and, to one measure or another, has entered into union with your being. What might your perceptive field of consciousness look like? How might the eyes of your understanding see and perceive differently? How might this equip and empower you to only do the Will of your Father? We are living in the days where God, once again, is answering Paul's prayer. We are in the days where the overcomers will have the abiding spirit of wisdom and revelation available to them. Living in the renewed mind, the spirit of wisdom and revelation are released through a specific process revealed in this passage. Hidden in plain sight, right in this passage, is the means through which the appearing of the abiding presence of the spirit of wisdom and revelation is experienced.

The phrase "in the knowledge of him" provides us with the key to experiencing Paul's prayer. The spirit of wisdom and revelation are held, "In the knowledge of him"—the information of the Kingdom—His knowledge. It's the information of the Kingdom that grows the renewed mind which is consciousness in the Kingdom realm. The spirit of wisdom and revelation are the conduits through which the Kingdom realm of consciousness are brought to our subjective experience. The appearing, in their abiding form, as opposed to merely presenting a revelation or some wisdom, become the catalyst for increasing awareness and personal experience in and of the Kingdom realm of consciousness. The measure in which the spirit of wisdom and revelation appear in their abiding form correlates with the measure in which our minds are renewed. In order for the spirit of wisdom and revelation to express themselves to you in their abiding nature, you must allow the information of the Kingdom to accomplish its work in you. The work I'm referring to is the construction of the renewed mind-the place where the abiding presence of the spirit of wisdom and revelation appear in your personal experience. This begins by committing to seek first the Kingdom-the knowledge of Him! As you do, trust the process. Have faith that Jesus' highest priority for you, seeking first His Kingdom, will yield such results. Be patient and resolute and prepare yourself for a transformation that transports you to a level of existence no eye has seen, and no mind has conceived. Jesus said:

"The words that I speak unto you, they are spirit, and they are life."
John 6:63b

In other words, "The life" information represents "tree of life" words. The substance within the information that Jesus presents is spirit in nature, therefore, as we receive the information from Him—the information of the Kingdom, we renew our minds with the essence of spirit, which is consciousness in and of the Kingdom. The essence of the Kingdom is Jesus Christ Himself. So, to have our consciousness moved into the Kingdom is to see Jesus as He is!

"Beloved, we are now children of God, and what we will be has not yet been revealed. We know that when Christ appears, we will be like Him, for we will see Him as He is."
1 John 3:2

Drops of oil fell on my wrists. The oil's aroma took me away to a large home. I knew the owners to be very wealthy and connected to movie production. I saw a lovely family who had what appeared to be healthy relationships. I looked at the father and saw he was not there. I thought, "Where is he?" The Lord responded, "He is not yet in the Kingdom." When he said this, a veil was lifted, and I saw unholy activity. The Lord continued, "You must tell the people they need to 'come up here.' They must enter the Kingdom, and then build community with Me. Without the foundation of the home resting in a Kingdom foundation, it rests on sand. The winds that are coming, the storm that is brewing will tear down communities outside My Kingdom."

An aroma filled my nostrils as I took a deep breath. I took another, then another. Suddenly, I was back at the throne. I felt like a computer receiving an information download. I asked, "What is going on?" I heard nothing. Silence remained for several seconds. Then I heard, "You have been given keys to build five communities." "What are they?" I asked. "The individual inner life, the family, Church, city, and nation." As he was sharing these, I felt a download. It didn't feel good, but the bad feeling quickly subsided. "What was that?" I asked. He responded, "That was lots of information."

I thought, "How can I get this out? There is no way." As I was thinking, "There is no way," the Lord said, "Don't think more highly of yourself than you ought to. I have others who will receive this download. Some you will lay hands on, while others I will deal with personally. Be careful who you entrust Kingdom information with. Fear not My child, it is My good pleasure to give you the Kingdom. This time you will not be alone."

I left this place and lay before the throne. My back began to hurt. A voice spoke, "You have carried weight you were not called to carry. I am removing the weight of worry, concern, and frustration of communities being built outside the Kingdom realm. Soon you will be placed in a community rooted in the Kingdom realm." I then had a vision that scared me. The vision caused me to realize that fear of rejection was lodged in my identity, and I asked for it to be removed. My heart galloped as my mind drifted. I became weak and hungry. Then I heard the Lord speak, "You have left your place in My Kingdom and have entertained desires not from me. I know that your desire to see authentic Kingdom community is from My heart but not everything in My heart I have given to you. Let Me have My desire for Kingdom community back." Immediately, I gave it to Him and agreed with Him. I became energized and felt the Kingdom within expanding.

I was led away in the spirit where I was shown millions upon millions of small foundations with no building materials on top. They were contained within one big foundation. Then I saw the little foundations being built upon. They were taking shape when I realized they were temples and understood them to be representing human bodies. The big foundation they were on was Christ. The voice spoke, "Take courage! All Kingdom knowledge of community learned outside the Kingdom; the King brings in as building material." When He was finished, I saw a flash so fast I didn't see what it was. I asked, "What was that?" I heard a voice, "That's the start of redeemed knowledge of community. All 'parts' of Kingdom knowledge is redeemable once a Saint is moved into the Kingdom." When He said this, I saw angels around the throne worshiping. A currency that I knew to be faith was exchanged for building material.

I was then whisked away to the inside of a computer monitor. There I saw information being downloaded so fast it looked like nothing I could describe. I heard the source of the information speak, "This is the Kingdom age. I am the spirit of Revelation. Information is different in this realm. Here, I open myself, and all that is within me is opened to you instantly. You now have access to me at the Lord's discretion." I wondered where I was and asked. He answered, "It's not for you to know where and when I choose to deposit the contents of my information. It's enough for you to know this is the Kingdom way." I remembered a verse that said, "Behold I am doing a new thing, something I've never done before." As I thought of that verse, I saw that word and passage come alive. It got up and approached me. I stood in anticipation, and the words spoke, "Now is the time. Eat and be satisfied." I swallowed and felt an angel touch my throat as contents began flowing into my stomach. I began crying, fell back and was before the throne.

As I pondered what just transpired, I acquired understanding from the spirit of Revelation. In this dimension, vision contains the whole of the revelation. Every time you see something in this realm, all the information contained in the vision is downloaded in you. (Since this experience, I prefer to say the revelation was "opened to me" rather than downloaded since it's quite possible the spirit of Revelation is within.) When I realized this, I was taken back to the "library" I visited earlier. I looked around, and it was in the same condition as before. As soon as I looked at the books on the ground, the pages began to grow like Jack's bean stalk in the fairytale. My heart erupted in excitement as I watched. I realized the ceiling was gone and the books kept growing and growing. I thought to myself, "This is going to go on forever!" A voice interrupted and said, "You are correct. I have been instructed to open the vaults of knowledge." When he said this, the right side of my head experienced a shooting pain, and I heard one of the loudest eruptions of praise before the throne. I had to get there to see what was happening.

Before the throne were ancient Creatures full of life. I could see they had all eaten from the tree of life. I asked what the eruption of praise was about when flashes of light startled me. I heard, "Heaven on earth is about to accelerate in human consciousness. All creation has been waiting for the knowledge vault to be opened. Now the sons of God will arise. Stay here and tell others." "Stay where and tell others what?" I replied. The voice responded, "Stay in 'pursuing only what you see the Father doing' and tell everyone to seek first the Kingdom." Then he joyously exclaimed, "The knowledge vault has been opened, and the spirits of Wisdom and Revelation are free to make their abode once again in man's heart." I was moved forward and to the left. I saw the spirit of Wisdom and Revelation dancing to a song with the lyrics "I love your Kingdom, in the influence of your Kingdom I will find rest in souls." Suddenly, I was deep into what looked like the heart of the Father. The surroundings were all resonating a sound—"I love your kingdom, I love, I love your Kingdom." When I got to the end, I realized it wasn't the heart of God. It was a single cell in a Saint. The cell was worshiping God for the abiding presence of the spirit of Revelation.

I began crying and thought, "How can this be? The body contains somewhere around 40 trillion of these." I noticed the size of the cell and all its parts worshiping. I became overwhelmed as vision of Isaiah 6 entered my mind. I saw the man. I saw the Lord, and He was high and lifted up. The Lord spoke, "Son of man, you will see even greater things than this. Go. Tell your family it's time to restore My temple." As He was speaking, the crystal clear river manifested to my right. I heard a voice declare, "Not yet. Stay focused on the task at hand." He knew of my desire to step into the river and drink of it. I turned away and heard a host of angels cheering on humanity, singing "and the temple is filling with the Glory of God! Fill the earth with the Glory of God!"

I was energized and became curious about the next level. My attention turned, and I saw the river again. I heard the Lord say, "You are moving ahead of me." As He spoke, I smelled the stench of what I knew was hell and felt its presence. I agreed, and the Lord said, "Keep your focus inward. My Kingdom within is where I want your eyes fixed. You cannot build community My way without My community established within." When He said this, I saw the words superposition and entanglement and heard a voice shouting, "Invade my way of thinking." Immediately, I was taken to an oasis where I was given heavenly bread I knew to be straight from an oven. The aroma opened earth, and I saw Eden established. I thought, "Where am I?" There was silence. Then I heard, "Tell everyone to seek first My Kingdom and My righteousness." I was then lead to the throne where I remained.

I was fed an energizing substance, but I knew it wasn't manna. It birthed anticipation of what I was about to hear. The spirit of Wisdom then downloaded information on Kingdom community development I could see was entitled "entering the promised land." As this information was made known to me, I became sorrowful over my inability to recognize the spirit of Wisdom as a female. Up to this point, I had perceived her as a male. She responded, "Don't be sad, everyone on earth has sin keeping them from seeing truth. Feel good you became aware, confessed, and behold; now you see." When she said this, a light flashed on the earth, and a voice spoke, "Seal this information for now. Soon you will be entering the Promised Land with a few Saints. Study the Promise Land in Scripture. I will open the eyes of those soon to enter with you so that union may be your catalyst." I became tempted to look into the future, but Wisdom prevented me. "Thank you, Wisdom. You truly are what Proverbs says about you." She responded, "Your acknowledgment of me is a testimony of the King's redemptive power. Never forget you are one thought away from falling like lightning from this place." It was then I saw Satan fall like lightning and awareness was opened to me. Wisdom continued, "As you see me nudging you to share information pertaining to Kingdom community development, do so. You will be established in trust towards certain family members soon. As your comfort level increases, let that be a sign I am ready for you." When she finished, I saw an expansion of Kingdom community beginning with an individual discovering the Kingdom community within. The expansion ended when the earth and heaven had become one. I felt privileged and honored when the spirit of Wisdom spoke, "The 'privilege' feeling was of the divine nature, the 'honored' feeling was from Satan." I saw it, agreed and heard her respond, "Be watchful for false honor. When you see it accept it, but acknowledge that all honor belongs to the Father of fathers." I agreed and bittersweet manna was placed in my mouth as I saw Satan get behind me. "Be alert; the Devil prowls around looking to inject his nature." I was lifted back in time to the wilderness where Jesus was tempted.

Jesus spoke, "You will need to know, no student is greater than his teacher. You will encounter Satan as he finds opportunity. You need to cry out for eyes to see and ears to hear." I knew He was referring to eyes and ears to "only do what I see my Father doing." I asked where I find such virtue and strength. Wisdom appeared and said, "You need wisdom. I will direct you after a season of testing. Those in the third rung must pursue their goal of only doing what you see the Father doing. The Isaiah 6:1 Saint is nearing emergence upon the earth in the remnant of pioneers." Suddenly winds from the North and South began blowing over me. "Wait," said Wisdom. I waited and was given liquid with living essence and began to declare, "Awake Northwind, awake South wind, blow over me." I heard rain falling and continued, "Let the winds blow." A door opened, and I saw the Holy Spirit enter chambers of the heart no man could identify. I saw Him taking out nasty and filthy things-things whose root system goes back to the Garden of Eden. I heard a choir singing "Have your way," as multitudes cried out to be refined like gold transmuted into white powder. I realized something and was told to seal it up and focus on the task at hand-only doing what I see the Father doing.

I saw a tornado forming over a sea. It had formed and was moving. Wisdom appeared beside me and turned me. She spoke, "Don't look at anything but the tasks at hand. Tell God's Saints both on earth and in Heaven on earth to get their eyes off all things not pertaining to the Whole." I thought, "This is a tall order. That means only 'seeking first the Kingdom' is acceptable activity for first rung Saints." I started to get discouraged when I remembered my perceived responsibilities versus God's Will. "See?" Wisdom responded. "The Word of God divides effectively." I agreed, and Wisdom continued, "Pray for the removal of all activity that wastes time and serves to inhibit the construction of the renewed mind." TV, Internet, entertainment, and all manner of foolishness entered my mind. Wisdom replied, "You are correct. Don't forget news, things related to economy, earthly government, politics and all other information communicated outside the confines of seeking first the Kingdom." I asked, "What about the election in America? She responded, "Give no thought. The LORD has set in office whom He has chosen." I knew not to ask who, but my flesh was tempting me. "The following election will be determined by the Saints." I cried out for mercy on America and heard the Lord speak, "Keep you and your family's task at hand. I will enlarge your family once I see you implementing your tasks at hand." Wisdom responded, "Your time with me here has ended for now. Keep your tasks at hand, and I will revisit you in this place later." I agreed and departed to the throne.

Thoughts for Kingdom Community Establishment, Development, and Growth

The first community in existence was God's creation in Genesis Chapter One. God created community in the Garden—the Kingdom realm on earth. Therefore Kingdom community is discovered in the realm of the Kingdom. We cannot begin to step into Kingdom community until a group finds themselves transported into the realm of Kingdom consciousness.

Before we introduce information designed to help build Kingdom community, I want to establish a foundation. Any good builder esteems the foundation above all. Without the foundation, all building is a waste of time, talent, and energy. Building Kingdom community is no different. Connecting and growing in relationship with the inner Kingdom is foundational to the effectiveness of expressing it outwardly. Connecting with and experiencing *"Christ in you"* is the first step to entering a collective Church expression of Kingdom community. Once you have connected with Him experientially, begin developing an intimate relationship. Increase your conscious contact and ask Him to open up His *"Kingdom within."* To increase times of intimacy with the King, you must intentionally put aside time to sit with Him. This often requires long periods of time in stillness, because in order to know God in our conscious experience we must cultivate inner stillness. As we will discuss in later chapters, stilling your mind, quieting your emotions, and disengaging from your Will is important to experiencing Christ and His Kingdom within.

Seeing the Kingdom within is essential to modeling collective Kingdom community. For those hungry for vision of the Kingdom within, I will tell you the only way to see the Kingdom is to seek it. You must make it your top priority to seek the information of the Kingdom. If you do, you will see the Kingdom in His timing. As you do, pay close attention to its attributes related to healthy community. Love, honor, respect, acceptance, communication, fellowship of depth, etc ... all centered on the King, are a few of the attributes you will discover. As you do, by faith take them into your community and begin, from the place of Heaven, allowing the Lord through you to establish them. Remember you are a Kingdom citizen. You're not from the earth; you're on the earth. You're not in the earth you're in Heaven. These are important distinctions necessary to establish in your thinking. My prayer is that you discover the Kingdom within so that you may become aware of the community of Heaven, which will empower you to effectively establish His Kingdom community on earth, as it is in Heaven. All activity of God on earth originates from the revealed mystery of Christ in you—the hope of influence.

The key ingredient to actualizing the attributes of healthy Kingdom community is the substance of Heaven materializing through the particular attributes. The key to materializing such substance is entering the Kingdom realm of consciousness. This happens only through the narrow road of seeking first the Kingdom. The first step in materializing the substance of Heaven is entering the field of the Kingdom of Heaven on earth. All words and activity flow from one of two fields—the field of the "parts" or the field of the "whole." Because the whole carries substance not found in the parts, we can have assurance that, in due time, the field of the whole will emerge in our field of consciousness. The more we remain in the environment of the whole, the more our words and actions will express the substance of Heaven.

Kingdom community is an enlarged and extended family expressing a substance that is not part of earthly community. That's not to say all earthly community is bad. In fact there are lots of good earthly communities but the enemy of the tree of life fruit is good fruit from the tree of the knowledge of good and evil. We no longer can afford to derive our sustenance from the tree of the knowledge of good and evil. The earth desperately needs substance only found from fruit eaten from the tree of life.

Let's go back to the idea of Kingdom community for a moment. The Bible is about a King, His Kingdom and Royal family. As His Kingdom expands out from the heart of man and touches another, community is formed. It ends with the whole earth filled with His royal family living in perfect harmony and union. From its conception to its completion is where we find ourselves. In order to co-labor with Christ to this end, we must understand the importance of taking in information relating to the Kingdom. We will never accomplish Kingdom community by studying and implementing community itself. You must have the field of the whole-the Kingdom—formed in your conscious experience first. The discovery and subsequent expression of Kingdom community must be rooted in the Kingdom realm of consciousness. You can no more hand a wheel to someone and convince them it's a car, than you can establish community and expect it to become what Christ created. Once you perceive the whole, then you will properly understand its parts. All Kingdom attributes flow out of the Kingdom. You can't take part of the whole and expect to produce its nature separate from the whole.

As we study the Kingdom and God begins revealing His Kingdom community, with His substance added, we realize it's more than we could have thought or imagined. Its culture, influence and unity can only be described through experience. My experience in June of 2013 enabled me to catch glimpses of this most treasured of Kingdom realities on earth as I saw Kingdom communities and their attributes being expressed. I can assure you, what I saw, no man can create. All our efforts in forming Church communities have grown temporary fruit at best compared to what I saw in these Kingdom communities. We must press into seeking first the Kingdom and patiently await our arrival into the Promised Land of the Kingdom realm on earth.

The following is a list of basic characteristics of community. Each characteristic is expressed either with substance from Heaven or not. Remember, when considering community carrying Kingdom substance, it's not the pursuit of community or community characteristics that manifests such substance but seeking first the Kingdom. Wait until you've been placed in the field of the Kingdom realm of consciousness before you consider the parts of the Kingdom and its community. For once you've been Kingdomized and brought into the field of Kingdom consciousness, the whole within the parts is opened to you. This results in perceiving the parts through the whole which ensures the appearance of the substance of Heaven coming alive in the parts.

1. A group of people is the most fundamental element of community. Kingdom groups have their foundation rooted in the discipline of seeking first the Kingdom.

2. Because community is territorial, it requires a definite locality. A Kingdom communities territory is the realm of Kingdom consciousness on earth.

3. Thought and belief is the glue that binds community. Without this essential characteristic, the sense of belonging is missing. Thought and belief is what separates one community from another. The key to God forming, growing, and expressing Kingdom community is the commitment to entering a "unity of mind" grown by seeking first the Kingdom.

4. Community exercises shared living. (Acts 2:42-47). For most, this is a difficult concept to accept or even imagine but one that will eventually become important for the Kingdom to be firmly rooted in the earth.

5. Community exists within a society. God's desire is to turn nations into Kingdom communities with the end result being the earth filled with the community of Heaven.

6. Kingdom community does require leadership such as Elders, Apostles, Prophets, Evangelists, Pastors, and Teachers. As these Kingdom community leaders come into their equipping identity, Jesus builds His Church and empowers the group to further Kingdom community and its effects on earth. All Kingdom leaders are subject to the Lord and must remain under His rulership.

7. Kingdom community requires specific leadership qualities (A teacher of the message of the Kingdom, not one who "lords" over the people, but one with humility, patience, gentleness, encouragement, who esteems others above his self, and gives godly guidance (1 Thes. 5:14, Gal. 6:2, Heb. 10:24, 25, and Matt. 22:37-40).

8. Each community member has a specific function according to the gifts given to them. They all are to be used. No one is better than another. The gifts are given by God through grace. (Rom.12:3-13).

Community is a group of people coming together with a common purpose. A measure of influence is created, determined by the scope and precision of the community's vision. As followers of Christ, the most effective purpose to unify around is seeking first the Kingdom. Walking in the purpose of seeking first the Kingdom becomes the vehicle of transportation into the Kingdom realm of consciousness. All the Kingdom "parts" expressed on earth begin sprouting in the soil of "seek first the Kingdom." The effectiveness of Jesus and the disciples' ministry was directly related to their purpose of community: expressing the attributes of the Kingdom in the individual and on earth. These expressions came into existence once they had immersed themselves, for an appointed time, in the message of the Kingdom. The outpouring of the Holy Spirit, on the day of Pentecost, was a response to those in the upper room engaged in community centered on the Kingdom. Heaven's community is birthed out of a group of people whose priorities are that of Heavens-the Kingdom. If you want to see the effects of seeking first the Kingdom, study the book of Acts. If you want to experience the life found therein, seek first the Kingdom with a group of like focus and dedication!

Kingdom community has identifying markers within it. The first and greatest is a common pursuit of Jesus' top priority for us: to seek first His kingdom. To seek something you must go hard after it. To seek first something is to have it consume more time and energy than anything. This can be measured and quantified by simply examining what occupies your time throughout a given day. When your thought life, time, and energy is consumed more with understanding the Kingdom, you are seeking first the Kingdom. When information of the Kingdom becomes the predominant field in which your psyche receives information, you can rest assured the effects of seeking first the Kingdom are set in motion. This discipline isn't woven into your identity overnight and requires patience and perseverance. It is, however, a road that takes you into the greatest place of existence the earth: the Kingdom realm on earth. It's where you were created to live out your existence. It's your inheritance and an everlasting place of rest and peace, despite the suffering and hardships that come with life. "Come to me all you who are weary and heavy laden and I will give you rest" by taking you into this place.

The Church has engaged in community, but its form and substance are different from the Book of Acts era. The present Church community is rooted in the carnal realm which limits expressions of Heaven on earth. There are two kinds of fellowship in the Bible. One is natural and earthy, while the other is spiritual and of the Kingdom. Under fellowship of the Kingdom, community is established immediately as two Saints walking in the Kingdom realm come in contact. The time it takes to develop a strong bonded relationship the earthly way is years and pales in comparison to the bondedness of spiritual fellowship in the Kingdom. Activity in the Kingdom realm of consciousness yields fruit very different from the same activity played out in the carnal realm of consciousness. Fellowship in the Kingdom realm throws off all limitations and opens the earth to Kingdom expressions not seen since the Book of Acts.

The attributes of community in the Kingdom are as follows: Union of the brethren instantaneously, or at least strong bonding. To the degree "death to self" and "unity of mind" has been actualized, is the degree of union amongst the brethren. A faith exchange will occur that generates an instant "building up of the body." This "faith-exchange," in conjunction with the fact that they are meeting in the Kingdom realm on earth, generates expressions of community the Kingdom way. This is one reason why Jesus always sent His disciples out together. We will discuss attributes of Kingdom community in the next book. For now my intent is to introduce Kingdom community in a general sense in hopes the reader begins moving towards it through the activity of seeking first the Kingdom.

Here is a summary of the three most important principles of Kingdom community:

1. Assembling and growing the community in the Kingdom realm of consciousness as you learn to distinguish between the Kingdom realm and the carnal realm.

2. The ascension process into the Kingdom realm requires the community to seek first the Kingdom as their primary focus. Seeking first the Kingdom grows the renewed mind which is conscious experience in the Kingdom. Not until the community enters the Kingdom realm do we begin devoting energy to Kingdom attributes and expressions.

3. The longer the community is engaged in the discipline of seeking first the Kingdom the more "unity of mind" takes place and is actualized. The actualization of "unity of mind" is the Kingdom's expressions upon the earth.

If you have participated in the earthly community paradigm, I want to encourage you to consider bringing what you learned to the Kingdom community. God is a redeemer and will bring every piece of earthly community attributes He can into His Kingdom. The most important decision you can make is to seek first the Kingdom daily. This single act, once your mind is renewed sufficiently, puts you in the same realm that the disciples of Jesus walked in. It places you in a position to grow and develop your consciousness in the Kingdom, not only in the community but in all facets of life.

During His ministry, Jesus gathered and developed a Kingdom community. By viewing His ministry in this light, we become empowered with understanding that shed's light on the model in which He used to awaken this Kingdom community to His culture. Simply put, Jesus gathered a group and taught them the message of the Kingdom. This postured them in the position of seeking first the Kingdom. This posture eventually transported the disciples, through the renewing of the mind, into Christ's realm of domain on the earth. This realm became their new space from which they lived—the Kingdom territory on earth. In a very real sense they were born again, only this birth was not of this world—the carnal realm of consciousness. Rather, through a change of mind from the carnal to the renewed, they were born into the Kingdom realm of consciousness experientially. What followed was an existence that expressed the culture and influence of Heaven everywhere they went.

> *"Very truly I tell you, whoever believes in me will do the works I have been doing, and they will do even greater things than these because I am going to the Father."*
>
> John 14:12

The Power of Community

1. The most powerful influence on earth is community. When people come together with "common unity," their "common unity" becomes established in the environment. What an environment contains is a reflection of the common union established under that environment. The United Nations calls itself the community of nations. Corporations create community among their employees. Cities and nations are communities. Churches, families, denominations, and religions are communities. The goal is not to just create communities, but rather to identify the right substance to come into common unity with. Heaven's substance is seeking first the Kingdom of Heaven. The first-century disciples entered community in the Kingdom realm of consciousness and were the last community brought together as the primary result of seeking first the Kingdom. Perhaps they were the only community to do so—until now. The common unity grown, developed, and realized by seeking first the Kingdom becomes the predominant community on the earth. On earth, the law of displacement esteems Kingdom community as superior. In

other words, when a Kingdom community is established on earth, its culture and social norms will trump all other culture formed by another community.

2. Community is the incubator of culture. Community is a group of people coming together whose common unity grows and develops culture. We must keep in mind an important principle taken from the life of Christ: *Jesus formed and established His community with those seeking first the Kingdom.* There are no rivals to the influence of a community who's established in the Kingdom realm. There are no rivals to a community whose common unity is formed while seeking first the Kingdom.

3. Community establishes and maintains culture. Community plays a role in impacting and imparting individual character traits.

4. To change your life, you must change your community. To change your life to reflect Heaven you must enter a common unity with the mind of Christ. This can only happen as you seek first the Kingdom. To change your culture to reflect Heaven you must change the common unity of the community to reflect the mind of Christ. This to is brought to pass as you seek first the Kingdom. Only this time, instead of seeking first the Kingdom alone, you seek first the Kingdom as a community. The image of Christ is best reflected upon the earth through a community seeking first the Kingdom. This was Jesus' prescribed model in the first century and needs to be ours today. There is great grace upon communities who commit to such an endeavor.

5. Nations manifest themselves in communities.

> *"Behold, you will call a nation you do not know, And a nation which knows you not will run to you."*
>
> Isaiah 55:5 NASB

Within every nation is the Nation of the Kingdom. As we come together in the common unity of seeking first the Kingdom, we enter the Kingdom realm of consciousness and "call a nation you do not know." Then "a nation which knows you not will run to you."

Mandate for Community

1. God's original and ultimate plan for earth was to rule the earth with the Kingdom community of Heaven. His means was to extend the "nation of Heaven" to earth—the Kingdom realm of consciousness realized and expressed through the renewed mind. In order to accomplish this we must bring conscious experience of the community and culture of Heaven on earth. We must enter a unity of faith by seeking first the Kingdom together. This process will grow the unity of mind which becomes the projector through which Kingdom culture is realized and then established in the earth.

2. God desires to fill the earth with the culture of Heaven. Culture is spread through the expansion of community. If you want to fill an area with culture, grow a community. If you want to fill an area with Heaven's culture, form a community rooted in the Kingdom realm and continue to seek first the Kingdom.

3. God's mandate is to express Heaven's culture on earth through the gathering together of community in the Kingdom realm. This transpires as the common unity is centered around the renewing of the mind with the information of the Kingdom. There is only one vehicle that transports you into the Kingdom realm of consciousness—the vehicle of seeking first the Kingdom.

Kingdom Community

1. A kingdom is a country. The bible is about a specific Kingdom, the Kingdom of Heaven. It contains the King's original thoughts, plans and ways of establishing the community of His country on earth. The Bible records God's blueprint for the Kingdom of Heaven brought back to life on the earth. The Bible also records God working with man in the carnal realm on earth. In the Kingdom age that is upon us, it becomes important that we distinguish the two, pursuing the blueprint, not God's help in our carnal realm. The carnal realm of consciousness has a problem, reaction, solution frame of mind. The Kingdom realm of consciousness has only solutions.

2. A country is an expanded community. As Christians, we are not members of a religion, we are citizens of a country—Heaven. Therefore we are an extension of Heaven's community. The purpose of Five-Fold Ministry is to equip the saints primarily by introducing them to their new identities as citizens in the Kingdom realm of consciousness. A drug addict leaving his culture for the first time carries baggage with him. As he enters the community of sobriety he discovers a new way of life. The quality of mentorship and discipleship determines the time it takes for transformation. The only way to successfully transition from one culture to another is to change your mind. Leaving the information associated with your old culture and receiving information found in your new culture is the means of bringing about the change of mind. This change of mind becomes the change that takes you from one realm of consciousness to another. Your present mindset reflects your present realm of existence. The new information you choose to dominate your thoughts and mind grows and develops patterns in your mind that bring the appearance of a new realm of existence that then takes over. The appearance of the new realm is in likeness to the information you choose to make your new priority. It's no wonder Jesus told us to seek first the Kingdom. He was providing us with the pathway that would lead us into His Kingdom realm on earth. He was leading us into the eternal realm of the Kingdom that is first within us, then expressed through us. Eternity, the Kingdom realm, is within you (see Ecclesiastes 3:11).

3. Kingdom community is common unity centered around values, laws ("let not these things be named among you …" Ephesians 5:3) standards, social norms, devotion, priority, and affection to Jesus and His Kingdom-all springing forth from the soil of seeking first the Kingdom of God and His righteousness. We don't esteem the values of the Kingdom above the discipline of seeking first the Kingdom. When we do we enter into foolishness as described by Paul … *"Are you so foolish? Having begun by the Spirit, are you now being perfected by the flesh?"* (Galatians 3:3 NASB). Seeking first the Kingdom is a safeguard keeping us from the works of the flesh. The same principle applies to esteeming the attributes of the Kingdom above the discipline of seeking first the Kingdom. The safest place to be

is seeking first the Kingdom and allowing the process to grow and develop the values and attributes of the Kingdom through the working of the Holy Spirit in you.

In conclusion, I do not doubt that Jesus loves humanity. I am, however, doubting the means through which the Church has attempted to present Kingdom community. One look at the present condition of culture and we can see that our ways are not God's ways. If they were, then what Jesus began in the 1st century, as it relates to how culture was influenced by the Kingdom realm, would have continued and even grown into the Kingdomization of the system of rulership which governs culture. A key to bringing back what Jesus began is rightly dividing one passage—John 3: 16. *"For God so loved the world"* is about Jesus loving, not us but the world-a system of rulership which has been taken over by Satan. Jesus' love is expressed in the manner in which He chooses when His Kingdom resurfaces in the system of rulership designed to govern culture. This is why He commanded us to seek His Kingdom above everything. When we do, we encounter the very essence of His governance through the world system. As this reality is set in motion, evangelism—His way—begins. Expressions of His love—His way—is realized by the receiver. It's time we stop trying to win souls and start seeking first the Kingdom. It's time we replace the hollow and deceptive presentation of the love of Jesus—which has been marinating in man's tradition far too long—and replace it with the authentic, radically transforming love of Jesus expressed once we enter community in the Kingdom realm. We must change our minds away from the ways of religion and man's ideas brought forth through the carnal man. We must acknowledge that the "good" we have practiced is fruit from the forbidden tree, reproducing forbidden fruit. In the realm of the Kingdom, all fruit that is not lasting is forbidden and of the flesh. We must come out from amongst man's way of extending community and position ourselves to receive God's way in the realm of the "Come up here." When we do, we can rest assured the greatest harvest in human history will be knocking at the Church's door. Let's commit to laying down the pursuit of the attributes of the Kingdom and pursue the Kingdom itself. This I believe is a major key to growing lasting fruit in the hearts of humanity. This is the key to growing Kingdom culture on earth as it is in Heaven.

Michael Sullivant, a man who's been aspiring to walk in Kingdom community for many years with his fellowship in Kansas City, eloquently speaks about the Kingdom way of community when he says:

"Koinonia, translated in English versions of the Bible is a central bonding agent that knits human hearts together in Jesus Christ and gives them a powerful sense of belonging to both God and one another. When believers who are living in the light of God open their hearts widely to each other in vulnerable communications, they feed Christ to each other in unique and special ways. The Holy Spirit travels the two-way streets between their hearts, and they enrich one another in the faith, hope, love, and joy that comes directly from the great heart of God through their individual personalities."

CHAPTER 3

Experiencing Christ and His Kingdom— Enter the Kingdom Within

I was led away in the spirit where I was shown revelation contained in Isaiah 6:1. Standing before me was a man that I knew represented both himself and the overcomers that would make up the Kingdom Church, having its existence in the Kingdom realm of consciousness. He was a dead man, though he lived. The life flowing out of him was no ordinary life, for it was life forged out of the fire of affliction that produced resurrected life. Suddenly I turned and saw the disciples sitting with Jesus alongside a river. I was told, "This is a period of time during the 40 days Jesus spoke to His disciples about the Kingdom in Acts 1." The Lord spoke, "There is a Kingdom talk before resurrection life and one after. I am bringing those I choose into resurrected Kingdom talk. They are to take the information revealed to you in Isaiah 6:1 and blow the trumpet of invitation."

Suddenly, a trumpet blew. I saw a door open and someone standing on the other side of the threshold saying, "Come up here, and I will show you things not yet known." I was taken through the door where there was another man. I knew this man came out of the previous man. The Lord spoke, "These are those who have entered My Kingdom. Look now how to operate up here." Appearing before my eyes was a vision of an ordinary day in the Kingdom. It was paradise on earth. I saw the Kingdom within the man. It was the eternal Kingdom encapsulated in a single body. This Kingdom was all that mattered to him as he was given over to searching it out. He had full faith and trust in the King establishing His throne on the earth. The Lord spoke, "Trust Me to lead you in establishing My Kingdom on earth. Take no thought of establishing My Kingdom on earth. Give yourself over to My Kingdom within. Seek first My Kingdom within."

I was then shown a man who was in superposition. He was always before the throne worshiping with innumerable multitudes. I also saw him carried to and fro throughout his day. I was told by a heavenly host I knew to be a messenger angel, "He is on assignment. To the degree you are yielded to Christ in you, is the degree you are on assignment." I felt a longing to be on assignment continually and expressed that feeling in thought. The Messenger read my mind and responded, "That is why you are here." I asked, "Where?" He responded, "The place of only doing what you see the Father do." Instantly I knew this was a dimension in Heaven—a realm in Heaven designated specifically for learning only to do what you see the Father doing. I thought, "This is the third rung." The Messenger responded, "Yes, you are correct in knowing the first and second steps as well. Tell the Saints."

Author's Note: The first step on the ladders rung is seeking first the Kingdom. The second is seeking His righteousness. Once the Lord has established enough groundwork in you through these first two steps, He will take you to this dimension. The maturity level at this point needs to be at a high level. No man can stand in this expressed measure of His presence unless the body and soul are purified to a certain degree. I have spent the past 3 days mostly in this level. My heart has been galloping, likely due to the weighty and holy presence here. The galloping heart I believe is due to the impurities still housed in my body and soul. I have been told I will be fine, but it is a reminder to stay humble, cry out for purification, and stay in the Lord's Will.

The Messenger continued, "Once you have reached this level in Kingdom living, the Lord will begin using you to awaken His Kingdom on earth." I heard a stern voice in the background, "Not until then." I thought, "What about all the 'Kingdom activity' on the earth presently? What about all the conferences and gatherings making claims of great moves of God coming—healings, miracles, etc." I thought to myself, "These people are not yet in the Kingdom. They don't even know what the Kingdom realm of consciousness is!" The Lord responded, "This is none of your concern. I am Lord of all.

You mind your task at hand and give no thought to anything outside My Kingdom within." I thought, "That's a tall order but yes Lord. Help me Holy Spirit."

Suddenly, I found myself back at the throne contemplating what had been said. I realized the season we are in—a season of seeking the Kingdom first. I knew this would be the field the Lord would bring His first harvest from. I saw a second season of seeking understanding of His righteousness and a third season of practicing "only doing what you see the Father doing." I heard a stern voice coming from the throne say, "Seal up information beyond this. Be careful who you share information beyond this. I have brought you a father in the spirit. Walk with Him." I realized there was silence in Heaven. At that moment I knew the Lord was finished speaking.

As I was being led from this place, something grabbed my arm and held me momentarily. I heard, "I am Wisdom and will be with the Kingdom-Dwellers. Take the inner Kingdom life information and teach others. I will be helping build what you saw in Isaiah 6:1. Remember the order: 1, 2, and 3. Seek first the Kingdom, seek first righteousness, and seek to only do what you see the Lord doing."

Thoughts on Experiencing God

Below is a chapter I wrote two months before my ten day experience in heightened awareness of the Kingdom realm of consciousness. I pray it be used as a catalyst to discovering the Kingdom that resides in you.

"When we come together to talk, or otherwise to act in common, can each one of us be aware of the subtle fear and pleasure sensations that 'block' our ability to listen freely? Without this awareness, the injunction to listen to the whole of what is said will have little meaning. If each one of us can give full attention to what is actually "blocking" communication, while also attending properly to the content of what is communicated; then we may be able to create something new between us, something of very great significance for bringing to an end the at present insoluble problems of the individual and of society."

David Bohm

Michael Gissibl

Entering the Kingdom Within—Establishing Isaiah 6:1 Within

I was led into the spirit where I knew I was standing inside a man. A man I knew to be the Isaiah 6:1 man. There were six characters residing in this man as I saw the inside of the man as territory occupied. The King of kings was by far the most significant character occupying the territory. He was living in the man's spirit. I saw the king of the body which was the man's spirit. I saw bondservants serving both Kings called mind, will, and emotion. I saw another bondservant serving both kings. I knew this bondservant was the body. I saw the King of kings, high and lifted up. I saw a son of God prepared to walk the earth as both King of kings and king for the King. This man was impressive beyond comparison and comprehension. I felt this was a model of what the Kingdom-dwellers look like. What the overcomers will soon be transformed into and emerge from the Kingdom realm on earth, ruling and reigning with Christ.

I heard a voice, "Write the keys to growing and developing the sons of man on earth as it is in Heaven. I will meet you here at an appointed time." I asked, "Where are we?" and heard in reply, "Not for you to know. I don't even know." I heard the Fathers voice, "Keep your mind on only doing what you see Me doing." I thought, "This is a hard teaching, who can do this?" At that moment Holy Spirit jumped in front of me and with a big smile replied, "Me! I need you to help Me get the word out! The Kingdom once was lost but now is found! Give sight to the blind, give hearing to the deaf, this is the favorable year of the Lord!" I smiled, and as He left, I thought, "This is the greatest person I've ever met. The life expressed through Him is so unique. So vibrant! This life source is nothing I've seen or experienced." My attention shifted as I became amazed at life in the Kingdom realm of consciousness.

As I was drifting away in amazement, I was arrested in thought. "Don't forget your assignment. Keep your bondservants enslaved. Your task at hand is more necessary than a tickle of your emotions. Remember you are in the dimension of 'I only do what I see my Father doing.'" I agreed and humbly bowed.

While attending college in 1994, I experienced a supernatural healing which shifted my attention from college life to growing a relationship with Jesus. I began spending hours reading the Bible, studying, and meditating. I frequented Bible studies, listened to worship music, and prayed often. I was touched by the living God which ignited a passion for knowing Him. A year later, I came across a number of books relating to experiencing God's presence. Watchman Nee's, *The Spiritual Man*, and *The Release of the Spirit* was most impactful as well as Brother Lawrence's, *Practicing His Presence*. These books laid a practical foundation of how to engage in a relationship with Jesus that is tangible and experiential. They also introduced keys to identifying and removing stumbling blocks to experiencing God.

Years later, I was the adult Bible school teacher at my Church where I established and taught a class titled, *Four Principles to Experiencing God*. Because of my psychology background and gift of compassion, I was also asked to become the male counselor for the Church. It became my emphasis to connect clients with Jesus through the four discipline's I was teaching. I also was leading home groups, all with topics centered on experiencing Christ. I say this to paint a picture of how involved I was in the practice and pursuit of experiencing His presence. I was living and reliving, teaching and reteaching the principles necessary to experiencing Jesus. This way of life not only firmly established the foundational principles in me, but afforded me numerous hours dedicated to experiencing His presence. About eight years into this adventure, I entered a season that took me into a radical period of accelerated intimacy with Christ. I believe a major catalyst to accelerated intimacy and experience of "Christ in me" was the conditioning of the mind that took place while engaged in the development of the discipline of practicing His presence. The development had two primary legs that walked me into what ultimately came to be known as discovering the Kingdom within. These two legs are learning and practicing—becoming a student of those who lived a life of experiential intimacy with Christ and practicing the principles that led them to be able to teach others.

It all began one evening while I was lying on my couch worshiping Jesus. My wife and kids had gone to bed. The four principles for experiencing God and His Kingdom within, the ones I will outline soon, had become an established and conditioned discipline for me. I had been reading two books—*Standing in the Council of the Lord* by Charlton Kenney and *Engaging the Revelatory Realm of Heaven* by Paul Davis. Both books, on a foundational level, deal with God's desire for us to experience and even abide in His presence. *Standing in the Council of the Lord* lays out a Biblical precedence for entering an actual place in the third Heaven for the purposes of receiving counsel. The premise of this argument is taken from Zachariah 3:7, a passage I had been studying for quite some time. It reads, "This is what the Lord Almighty says: 'If you will walk in obedience to me and keep my requirements, then you will govern my house and have charge of my courts, and I will give you a place among these standing here.'" According to Kenney's argument and my understanding, God was offering Joshua a place in the council room in Heaven.

Author's Note: There is one other significant piece of information worth mentioning. I had been spending time with Bob Jones, a prophet who had been accessing the third heaven regularly and began teaching on it. I was at a Morning Star Ministries luncheon where Bob was teaching on Revelation 4:1:

> *"After this I looked, and there before me was a door standing open in heaven. And the voice I had first heard speaking to me like a trumpet said, 'Come up here, and I will show you what must take place after this.'"*

Once he completed the teaching, he invited us to come up, and he would pray for us. I went up for prayer, he laid his hands on me, but nothing happened experientially. After the meeting, I had lunch with him, and it was at that moment I knew something had happened. As we finished lunch and were about to go our separate ways, he looked at me and said, "I see you are like a World War II airplane sitting on an aircraft carrier, pulled back, ready to be launched." I said, "Thank you," wrote it down and went on my way. Fast forward a couple months where I was in my family room spending time with the Lord.

With this revelation marinating in my spirit man and worship springing out of my being, suddenly faith came to me. In the blink of an eye, I had strong conviction in the ability to access Heaven like Zachariah and Revelation talked about. Instantly, out of nowhere, Poof! There it was. I left my family room and found myself in the third Heaven, standing before a door about 10 feet tall and 5 feet wide. This place was astonishing! I had never felt the presence of the Lord like this, let alone experienced a place so majestic. It changed my understanding of "experiencing His presence" forever. It greatly expanded my idea of "divine" and "Holy" and formed a new belief system within me.

As I stood before this door, I became overtaken by its majesty. I found myself focused on the beauty of the color and the substance coming out from the color. I believe the door was made of the precious metal gold that carried divine substance in it. Suddenly the door opened. As quickly as it opened, it closed. This happened about as fast as someone's ability to open and close a door. What I saw in that split second was like nothing I'd ever seen. The purity and holiness of the experience left such an imprint on me it caused me to be unable to voice my adoration in worship for nearly ten years. The sound coming out of me as I worshiped was so unholy compared to the holiness of that moment, I chose to be non-vocal during times of worship. I continued to worship, just not expressing myself vocally. This proved to be a bigger blessing than I realized because it forced me to turn inward during worship, providing more opportunity to connect with Christ in me. The longer I remained in this discipline, the deeper, more intimate our relationship became. It also developed disciplines in me that made my relationship with Christ more meaningful in experience.

Back to the experience before the door. The holiness of the experience, coupled with my unholiness, was so terrifying it seemed like if I spent a millionth of a second longer in this place, I would turn to ash. I felt I would disintegrate into nothing. Everything in me resonated fear and utter terror. The light emanating from the room was blinding, though I could see. It consumed not only my vision but my entire being. This light wasn't coming from a particular area within the room; it consumed the room. It took up the entire room which was incalculable. I couldn't see anything but this divine light. Its brightness was all consuming. Nothing on earth or in Heaven compares to it. The color was a white gold and translucent in nature. Again, no color in our world possessed the qualities it contained. Even now as I relive the moment, words fail to capture the true essence and nature of the experience.

What happened, where was I, and what was the light behind the door? I don't know for sure. My thought is it was the throne room of Heaven, and the light was what emanated out from the throne of God— the essence of His nature. I'm not sure, but for the purposes of this chapter, it's not important. The point I want to emphasize is the fact that I had, for the first time, experienced God in an extravagantly new way. It had produced a hunger and thirst for Him that still propels me to seek out the unsearchable riches of Christ. I attribute, to a large degree, my persistent discipline of "experiencing Christ within" and genuine desire to know Him, to the reason why I had this experience. There are disciplines and principles necessary to enter into a relationship with Christ beyond the ordinary and mundane. Although I am in no way assuring you will enter into such experiences, I am confident that putting the principles laid out in this chapter into practice will empower you to deeper levels of experiencing Christ and His Kingdom.

For the next two years, I had experiences in the third Heaven daily. None were as magnificent as the above mentioned, but nonetheless, I engaged heavenly dimensions daily. The day "faith came to me" on my couch empowered me to access these realms of existence unencumbered. These experiences would prove to be an important tool that developed and helped shape my relationship with Christ. They also brought my intimacy with Him to new levels, not to mention my "pursuit of Christ" meter went off the charts. I began spending up to 15 hours a day with Him. Sometimes, after everyone in my home went to bed, I would spend 8 to 10 uninterrupted hours in the Lord's presence, many of them engaging the revelatory realm of Heaven. I was overtaken by the feelings of love and acceptance radiating from Jesus as I tried to reciprocate my affections. The atmosphere of Heaven is saturated with divine love-a love that carries substance only found in Heaven. All the heavenly beings I encountered during these two years exhibited similar expressions of love and acceptance. I was enveloped in a peace that surpasses understanding. The love emanating from these beings was attractive and even transferring to a degree. I knew the content of this love was transforming, all the way to the DNA level. My confidence in Jesus' love for me and acceptance of me became firmly established as shame and guilt began diminishing. I became fixated on experiencing His presence as long and as often as I could.

During these two years, I estimate spending somewhere in the neighborhood of 2800 hours engaging the revelatory realm of the third Heaven and interacting with heavenly hosts. An additional 5000 or more hours were spent in conscious communion with Christ in me. I encountered hundreds of angels, many rooms in Heaven and countless awe-inspiring experiences. Just living day to day life, my spiritual eyes were opened more than ever as I encountered angels working in the Kingdom realm on earth quite frequently.

Author's Note: Despite all this, my character was not being transformed like I would have thought. Later on, I discovered a principle; to immerse yourself in the heart of God is not the highest priority of Jesus. Immersing yourself in His mind is the supreme pursuit. What we receive in experience from Christ and His Kingdom can only be maintained as we take on the mind of Christ. Without the renewed mind, we do not carry what we receive in the manner in which God designed for us. When we seek first the Kingdom, we are seeking first His mind. Sure we encounter His presence and enter moments of affectionate intimacy with Him, but the transforming power comes when the information of the Kingdom renews our minds. This is important to keep in mind, in light of the addictive nature of His presence and the degree of satisfaction we experience while in it. We love God's presence because of what it does for us but where are those that will sacrifice to understand His mind! Those will become the overcomers that will abide in the realm of the *"Come up here."*

For two solid years, I grew in my understanding of the nature, character, and heart of Father God. I don't want to get off subject, but I need to let you know how the two years ended. I became so proud and arrogant from these lofty experiences that the Lord rebuked me. He took away my freedom to engage the revelatory realm of Heaven in 2005, and for almost ten years I experienced a dry time of spiritual awareness and experience. He didn't leave me and my inner life with Christ was not hindered. He simply took away access to places reserved for the humble at heart. Little did I know it would lead me into a season of learning about His thoughts and ideas that would turn out to be equally as important as discovering His heart. These places are reserved for those who seek first the Kingdom long enough to allow the information to renew their minds. You see, receiving the mind of Christ without His heart will always produce pride (1 Cor. 8:1—knowledge puffs up) and a misrepresentation of His nature. Carrying the heart of God without His mind keeps the establishment of His Kingdom on earth from happening and creates a movable prison, enslaving us to satisfying the lusts of the flesh with the attributes of His presence. We need His mind and heart, direction and character, His ways and attributes.

As I mentioned earlier, my first assignment as a Church elder was teaching a class whose content was largely taken from Watchman Nee's book, *Release of the Spirit*. I wanted people to experience God the way I had and Watchman's book, as far as I knew, was the only pathway that might accomplish this goal. When the leadership offered me a teaching position, I jumped on it and eagerly prepared a class I will briefly outline. It is my prayer you pick up these principles and begin cultivating an intimate relationship with the Lord and His Kingdom within. The following is a proven technique, aiding the individual's ability to "be still and know (through experience) that I am God."

Author's Note: Keep in mind, we are living in the Kingdom age. This is an age where the Lord is restoring the years the cankerworm has eaten. He is speeding up time. I believe, as you apply these principles, in conjunction with seeking first the Kingdom, you will not have to spend years cultivating the disciplines. Although there is no way to short-circuit the ways of God, I believe the Kingdom age is an era where things are sped up. Having said this, don't rush through this time of development. Enjoy the journey. Expect Jesus to meet you. Anticipate encounters with the Living God. A God that loves and accepts you perfectly, just the way you are. Seek the Kingdom within. Set your affections and intentions on developing an intimate relationship with this God that loves you unconditionally, and know this- your pursuit of Him is but a reflection of His pursuit of you! Settling into His will makes room for transformation His way!

Throughout history, God has always partnered with man to accomplish His purposes. Hearing and experiencing God is no different. Although He is with us to empower us as it relates to "our part," He nevertheless requires us to act. Then there is the sovereign part He plays-things only He can do. Establishing the practice of habitually leaning on Holy Spirit for strength is a key to hastening any work of the Lord. It's a balance of racing towards a goal and ceasing the labor of racing that is Heaven's perfect balance for us. The author of Hebrews said it wonderfully:

> *"Let us, therefore, strive to enter that rest."*
>
> Hebrews 4:11a

I pray the Holy Spirit empowers us to work hard at not working, in order that Christ and His Kingdom may be formed in us and expressed through us more perfectly.

CHAPTER 4

Four Principles for Experiencing Christ and His Kingdom Within

"Be still and know that I am God."

Psalm 46:10

The word "know" here is the same word used to describe Adam and Eve's intimate sexual experience in Genesis 4:1a—*"And Adam knew Eve, his wife, and she conceived …."*

It is my prayer for you, dear reader that the following principles become a springboard for you to enter an intimate relationship with Christ, resulting in the experiential discovery of the Kingdom of God within you.

> *"The mystery which has been hidden from the past ages and generations, but has now been manifested to His saints, to whom God willed to make known what is the riches of the glory of this mystery among the Gentiles, which is Christ in you, the hope of glory."*
>
> Col. 1:26, 27

> *"Now having been questioned by the Pharisees as to when the kingdom of God was coming, He answered them and said, 'The kingdom of God is not coming with signs to be observed; nor will they say, Look, here it is! Or, There it is! For behold, THE KINGDOM OF GOD IS WITHIN.'"*
>
> Luke 17:20-21

As long as we believe the external world is more impactful and real than the internal world, we will find our existence in this world's system. As soon as we catch the revelation that, in fact, the internal world is far superior in every way to the external world, then we are given opportunity to enter the realm of existence we were created for—the Kingdom realm!!

One: Dividing Soul and Spirit

"For the word of God is alive and active. Sharper than any double-edged sword, it penetrates even to dividing soul and spirit, joints and marrow; it judges the thoughts and attitudes of the heart."
Hebrews 4:12

An important step toward experiencing Christ and His Kingdom in us is the separating of man's soul and spirit. Since God is Spirit, we connect with Him Spirit to spirit. The spirit of man is our communal capacity with the Spirit of Christ. The spirit of man is the primary antenna that receives the signals God communicates to us. When sin entered the human body, man's soul and spirit became intertwined with the soul taking dominion. As long as man's soul rules him, which is his mind, will, and emotions, he is subject to his flesh. The Living Word needs to dethrone the soul from its place of dominion. Once we are willing, the first step in the process is separating the two. This action awakens our ability to discern soulish activity from spiritual. This division enables us to see activity within us and determine which nature— the soul or spirit —is leading, guiding and ruling. Additionally, the separation empowers the believer's spirit, in union with Christ's Spirit, to have rulership over the inner life. This was and still is God's original intent for man. *"He who is slow to anger is better than the mighty, And he who rules his spirit, than he who captures a city"* (Proverbs 16:32).

Ever-increasing degrees of union with Christ cannot take place until this separation occurs. Once it does, we can begin the process of becoming co-heirs with Christ not only in our inner life but in the Kingdom realm on earth. This will only be accomplished as we begin and continue entering into intimate communion with Christ. Let me emphasize: When man's spirit, in conjunction with Christ's Spirit is ruling our inner life, we are one step closer to becoming an instrument of change on earth as Heaven designed. "The one who rules his spirit is stronger than those that capture a city" implies cities will be taken by those who rule their spirit. It's essential we not transfer our priority to capturing cities and remain focused on ruling our spirits. The inner life is where our attention must be fixed. All authority has been given to Christ. He is the one, not only empowering us but determining when and how much power to express through us.

Jesus, the Word made flesh, and the Bible are the two instruments Scripture teaches will bring about the desired separation of soul and spirit. Revelation and His presence also are effective instruments of separation. This division is important in that it empowers us to have discernment as well as brings potential for unbroken communion with the Lord. Remember, God is Spirit, and those that connect with Him do so Spirit to spirit. As we ask Jesus to divide our soul and spirit, He hears our petition and responds. Likewise, as we read "the word," its living and active power contains a soul-spirit separating quality. The more separation there is, the easier it is to distinguish soulish activity from spiritual. Additionally, the easier it becomes to experience Christ.

> *"Therefore, since we are surrounded by such a great cloud of witnesses, let us throw off everything that hinders and the sin that so easily entangles."*
> Hebrews 12:1a

Your spirit man has senses like your natural man. However, your natural man has covered them up. We must "throw off" our soul, making room for our spirit to live and move and have dominion over the inner life. The fall of man made room for substance from Satan which dethroned the spiritual man, producing a carnal nature that plays out its existence largely through the soul's activity. The unregenerate soul's primary objective is to suppress the life of the spiritual man in order to remain in control. The flesh truly does war against the spirit. Separation produces a sort of practical birth in the sense that it brings to life spiritual senses and empowers the spiritual man to take back dominion. This uncapping or rolling away of the stone does not constitute the new birth; rather it affords us the opportunity of experiencing life within the new birth. Separation also levels the playing field of your inner life, affording you the opportunity to no longer let flesh have dominion.

Another way of illustrating this separation is looking at the Greek word for transformation which is metamorphosis. This word paints a beautiful picture of a butterfly being confined in its cocoon before breaking through the layers in order to live according to its created end. Previously, it was enveloped and surrounded by the cocoon, which was holding it back from its purpose in another realm— the air. Once separation took place, and the butterfly "threw off" it's covering, new identity was realized, and newness of life in another realm was experienced and lived out.

Much like your natural senses discern the natural world mostly through sight and sound, so too do your spiritual senses in your inner world. Having spiritual senses "turned on" or enlightened empowers you to determine where thoughts originate, whether your spirit or soul is ruling and all other necessary bits of information required for a Christ-centered inner life. Additionally, this opens the door for you to view, outside of your soulish self, how much sanctification is needed. The heart of man is desperately wicked and deceitful above all things. No human is given a glimpse into this truth apart from the separation of soul and spirit. As you begin discerning your intentions and discovering your motives, remain humble and prepare yourself for a battle. Your flesh will not surrender without a fight. It is my experience that by keeping your eye on the prize, entrance into the Promised Land of the Kingdom realm of consciousness, you will find the process more tolerable. The Lord knows the battle ahead of time and equips us with tools for victory —none more attractive than glimpses of the Kingdom within, in the form of conscious experiences'. It is my prayer that as you put into practice these disciplines, the Lord captures you with His astonishing Kingdom.

One final note regarding the separation of soul and spirit. When Paul said to the Church at Corinth, *"though our outward man perish, yet the inward man is renewed day by day,"* (2Corinthians 4:16) he was distinguishing between the soul and spirit. As our soul separates from our spirit, we become empowered to distinguish between the "perishing" of our soul and the "renewing" of our spirits. This presents us with an opportunity to rejoice during our afflictions, knowing the afflictions are meant to bring death to our carnal life flowing from our soul. Furthermore, through intentional focus, we are given a glimpse into the renewing of our spirits.

Two: Quieting/Stilling the Mind

Helpful terms to familiarize yourself with:

A. *Self-talk*—an ongoing internal conversation you have with yourself.

B. *Metacognition*—the ability to step outside of yourself for the purpose of examining yourself.

C. *Intrusive thoughts*—thoughts that originate outside yourself that come from the atmosphere of the carnal realm.

Psychology has coined the term "self-talk" to refer to the ongoing internal conversation we have with ourselves. Our carnal minds are always active, producing about 60,000 words a day. Many of these words originate from an established belief system that produces brain chemistry. Such a system causes automatic thoughts to flow out of the mind perpetually. This conditioning patterns our brains with the essence of what makes up our conscious experience. The Bible calls these automatic thoughts "strongholds." Like learning to ride a bike, what becomes established becomes automatic. We talk with ourselves constantly, but rarely become aware of the conversations since they originate primarily in the sub-conscious—the area of "established belief." These established beliefs form our identity, place us in a primary field through which we view conscious experience, and determine what dominates our awareness. In order to connect with these strongholds, we must step outside of ourselves, quiet our emotions, and begin searching for the stream of "conversations" within. Once we become aware of our self-talk, we can see what types of conversation we're engaged in and make adjustments accordingly. Our goal is to be conformed to the image of Christ. A major step to this end is changing the way we think. The following are proven steps to guide you through the process, leading to a stilled mind, resulting in a conscious connectedness with Christ and His Kingdom—Spirit to spirit.

Authors Note: *"We take every thought captive"* (2 Cor.10:5). *Metacognition* is a term used to describe one's ability to step outside of themselves. In order to begin the discipline of taking thoughts captive, or as I like to say–"think about what you're thinking about"–we must begin observing our thoughts outside of ourselves. To step outside of yourself, engage your will and intent toward this end. Trust the Lord to empower you by dividing your soul and spirit. This is a major catalyst to perceiving yourself from your spirit man.

Having dominion over "self-talk," empowers you to still your mind. This is an important step toward experiencing God and living in His Kingdom realm of consciousness. Awareness is the first step to mastery. Therefore, test to see how long you can stop thinking by timing yourself. When I taught my students this principle, I encouraged them to buy a stopwatch. Although it's not necessary, you may find it useful. This exercise brings awareness of your self-talk by forcing you to find it within. You can't test something without first identifying it. It also makes clear how much mastery your subconscious self-talk has over you. In my experience, most people initially have a hard time stilling thoughts for more than three or four seconds. Don't let this discourage you. Persistent practice yields results—usually rather quickly. If possible, get into the habit of practicing throughout the day. Within a couple weeks, you will likely find that your "still time" has increased dramatically. Throughout the years, my students found themselves able to stop self-talk for up to a minute or two within a few weeks. The amount of time spent practicing is key. The longer you still your mind, the better listener in the spirit you become and the deeper the union is experienced with Christ. A stilled mind, coupled with a Will to seek Christ and His Kingdom within, yields great returns.

An unsanctified, active mind is enmity against God and will divert attention away from the experience and practice of conscious experience of Christ and His Kingdom. I want you to focus on your subconscious self-talk but not to the exclusion of your conscious thoughts. It is just as important you discipline yourself to still all thoughts. However, initially give your attention to becoming aware of your subconscious self-talk when possible. All self-talk flows out of the carnal mind which becomes the tether that binds you to the carnal realm of consciousness. Once self-talk ceases and your intent is placed on the spirit life, you begin growing a connection to Christ and His Kingdom that, over time and diligence, unties you to the carnal realm and connects you to the Kingdom realm. 2 Corinthians 10:5 states:

> *"We demolish arguments and every pretension that sets itself up against the knowledge of God, and we take captive every thought to make it obedient to Christ."*

You can't take captive thoughts until you become aware of them. Think about what you're thinking about! As you discover thought outside that which pertains to seeking the Kingdom, engage your will against them. Replace the thought with one that originates from the renewed mind which is part of your spirit man. You will know these thoughts because they are all connected in one way or another with the Kingdom. A safe barometer to gauge for whether your thoughts are surfacing from your self-talk or your renewed mind is; firstly, does the thought have to do with seeking first the information of the Kingdom—the knowledge of God? Secondly, does the thoughts line up with Philippians 4:8 (NIV)?

> *"Whatever is true, whatever is noble, whatever is right, whatever is pure, whatever is lovely, whatever is admirable--if anything is excellent or praiseworthy--think about such things."*

Each time you're engaged in "stillness of mind" and your self-talk starts up or conscious thoughts arise, resist them, and don't give up. Quiet your mind and get right back into stillness. Rise up in your spirit and subject your mind to it. The more you practice, the longer the stillness becomes. The longer the duration of stillness, the more you will experience connectedness with Christ. Invite the Lord to work with you. Ask Holy Spirit for divine empowerment. Let Jesus know you want Him to reveal His presence and Kingdom to you in a personal way and speak to you during these times. Invite Him to reveal His nature, character, mind, and Kingdom to you. There is no encouragement better than experiencing the Living God! Ask Holy Spirit for strength, perseverance, and courage. Invite Him to help during the process and empower you to victory. Continual dedication ultimately leads to a mastery of the mind, empowering you to shut it down ad infinitum. This opens a whole new relational dimension that strengthens and unifies your accord with Jesus and His Kingdom. I say this as an encouragement for you to press into the discipline of practicing His presence in His Kingdom. It is my experience that in time, you will effectively be able to live out your days with a stilled mind, in union with Christ, spirit to Spirit.

Once you're able to still your mind for more than 30 seconds or a minute you're ready for the next step. This involves discovering God in your spirit man. Your spirit and the Holy Spirit are in union and the Kingdom is in the Holy Spirit, therefore, your spirit man resides in the Kingdom which is within you. Becoming aware of this place empowers you for conscious experiences in the Kingdom and ultimately habitation within this most desired of all Nations—the Kingdom of Heaven on earth. I believe it was Paul Keith Davis who coined the phrase "engaging the revelatory realm of Heaven." This statement paints an accurate picture of a dimension in space/time that God desires for us to access and abide in. First, we must learn the art of stilling our minds and emotions. Since this revelatory realm is in Heaven on earth, when we step into this type of meditation we are availing ourselves to the Kingdom. In this place, all limits of experience with Christ and His Kingdom are thrown off. I believe Jesus remained perfectly in this place and is where "union with Christ" is found, nurtured, developed, and sustained. Although we will never reach perfection, it is a worthy endeavor to pursue ever-increasing union with Christ. If the Bible exhorts us to pray without ceasing, then it is without question possible to enter union with Christ, in His Kingdom, without ceasing.

Begin setting your intentions on listening for and experiencing God's presence. Remember, you are meeting Christ in His Kingdom, so don't be surprised if you encounter Kingdom sightings. Keep in mind; you are in a relationship desiring greater levels of conscious experience and transformation within the Kingdom realm. Lay aside all concern of being deceived and trust your All powerful, All-loving Heavenly Father to keep you from such deception. It was the Lord who put this desire for Him in you in the first place. He wants you to come into the secret place and be with Him more than you, so settle all issues. Try to condition your mind that you're entering territory of another realm—the realm of the Kingdom. You're not looking to connect with Jesus on your terms, in your world. Rather, you're embarking on a journey into the world of the Kingdom realm of consciousness within you. Anticipate God enlightening the eyes of your understanding in the Kingdom within.

> *"Ask, and it will be given to you; seek and you will find; knock, and the door will be opened to you. For everyone who asks receives; the one who seeks finds; and to the one who knocks, the door will be opened.*

Which of you, if your son asks for bread, will give him a stone? Or if he asks for a fish, will give him a snake? If you, then, though you are evil, know how to give good gifts to your children, how much more will your Father in heaven give good gifts to those who ask him!
Matthew 7:7-11

Lay down your agenda, ideas, and desires. Let all energy be consumed in your intentional pursuit to experience the Living God in the everlasting Kingdom within. God has set eternity within you (Ecclesiastes 3:11). Jesus made it clear that the Kingdom of God was within you and it was the Fathers good pleasure to give it to you. Consider your "stilled mind" an open doorway into the experience of practicing conscious contact with His Kingdom and His presence. I want to emphasize the importance of intentionally seeking the Lord and His Kingdom during your "stilled mind" times. It is just as important to the process as anything. Engage your will and set your affections and attention on things above.

The Renewed Mind: A Catalyst to the Rise of the Overcomers

As mentioned earlier, Psychology has identified a stream that flows from outside of us. They use the term intrusive thoughts to identify these thoughts. Psychology also describes the continual flow of thoughts from within as self-talk. These two streams of thought are responsible for the formation of the carnal mind and ensure its continued effect on our consciousness being rooted in the carnal realm. As we seek first the Kingdom, we provide our brain with the information responsible for growing the renewed mind. Simultaneously we are collapsing the carnal mind. Part of that collapse includes the eventual end to our stream of self-talk, empowering us to live out of a stilled mind.

Kingdomology, the study of the Kingdom, identifies a stream of thought that flows outside of us, which I term "intended thought." In the Kingdom realm of consciousness, the renewed mind enters into a relationship with the Kingdom realm whereby a stream of thought begins flowing from Heaven. Starting as tributaries, the living water increases its flow the longer we remain engaged in receiving the information responsible for growing and developing the renewed mind. The following is the process of preparing the renewed mind for the steady flow of Heaven's thoughts.

a. Collapsing the carnal mind—the carnal mind begins its descent the moment we seek first the Kingdom. Each moment we engage in the receiving of the information of the Kingdom, we are dismantling the carnal minds assembly. Additionally, the moment we entertain fragmented information, information outside of the confines of seeking the Kingdom, we engage in the construction and upholding of the carnal mind. The tension of upholding and collapsing the carnal mind is a good starting point, but a change needs to take place eventually. That change is the transition where you begin taking in more information of the Kingdom than you do all other information. Jesus referred to this as seeking first the Kingdom. Seek, as your top priority, the information of the Kingdom. This is accomplished each day we receive 50.1% of our information while seeking the Kingdom. Distinguishing between the two streams of information allows us to see which mind is being fed; the carnal mind or the renewed mind. Theoretically, if we receive 50.1% or more of information flowing from the field of Kingdomology, sooner or later we will be transported into the realm of the renewed mind which is consciousness of the Kingdom realm.

   Great acceleration in the collapse of the carnal mind begins the moment we step over that threshold. Even greater acceleration will happen as we open schools of Kingdomology and begin graduating students who've given themselves over to the study of the Kingdom for lengthy periods of time. Jesus revealed and modeled His highest goal for us through His relationship with His disciples. To be fully given over to a life of seeking the Kingdom, hour by hour, day by day, year by year—this is the invitation. The disciples left everything to surrender to a life as a student of the information of Jesus—the message of the Kingdom. When they wanted to leave such a commitment momentarily, Jesus would challenge them by saying things like, "Let the dead bury their own dead. You, however, go and proclaim the kingdom of God." (Luke 9:60) Or, "No one who puts his hand to the plow and then looks back is fit for the kingdom of God."

b. Stopping self-talk—"The weapons we fight with are not the weapons of the world. On the contrary, they have divine power to demolish strongholds." A stronghold of the carnal mind is self-talk. Self-talk is a tributary flowing from the carnal mind made up of conditioned patterns of thought that are played over and over in our subconscious mind. Of the thoughts that make up our self-talk, 90% are repeated every day and form the basis of conformity to this world system—the carnal realm of consciousness. Because most self-talk flows out from our sub-conscious, most never become aware it even exists. Nevertheless, the thoughts are still there, forming the basis of what we see, hear, feel, and even how we behave.

The sword of the Spirit is the weapon that demolishes self-talk. The sward of the Spirit is the word of God-the information of the Kingdom. Receiving the information of the Kingdom is like a sword slowly cutting off the life source of self-talk, the carnal mind. Or like an ax at the root of a tree, so too is the steady flow of Kingdom information. Each measured intake of Kingdom information yields the strike of the ax upon the root system of the carnal mind. As damage to the carnal mind continues, the life source of the self-talk is being cut off. John the Baptist could prophesy, "The ax is already at the root of the trees, and every tree that does not produce good fruit will be cut down and thrown into the fire" because Jesus had arrived with the message of the Kingdom—the information responsible for cutting down the life sources of the carnal mind.

As the carnal mind collapses so too does your self-talk. Although your carnal mind will never become fully disbanded in this life, your self-talk does. This opens your self up to the discipline of stilling your mind at deeper levels. A stilled mind is a prerequisite to articulating the flow of information from Heaven, the intended thoughts of Heaven received by either your spirit or the renewed mind.

c. Entering the discipline of a stilled mind with your intentions set on receiving from the Lord moves you in a posture to encounter the Living God. The general state of the renewed mind lives in a state of rest. Disengaged from all activity, the renewed mind waits for a flow from Heaven. Inactivity is no problem for the renewed mind because the waiting is simply an opportunity to enter into heart to heart fellowship with your lover, the King of this marvelous Kingdom within. Living life through the renewed mind limits all activity to being a lover or listener. The only activity of doing is once you've seen what the Father's done.

d. Growing the renewed mind is a process that never ends. Receiving the information of the Kingdom is the foundation of all life flowing in and from the renewed mind. Until the maturity level of the renewed mind reaches a certain point, all attention needs to be given over to seeking first the information found in the field of the Kingdom. Once the self-talk of the carnal mind ceases and you begin entering the Kingdom field of consciousness, there comes a point where the spirit of Wisdom and Revelation are awakened to you. As they begin entering and appearing to the eyes of your understanding, know that you have entered the Kingdom realm of consciousness on a deeper level. This is a critical time to examine yourself, making sure you are humbling yourself and carrying your cross daily. Embracing all hardships as a tool to keep you anchored in the Kingdom realm is a wise mindset to condition your way of thinking. Keep seeking first the Kingdom but add another discipline to your routine. Fix your attention on your mind and spirit, quietly waiting for communication from the King and/or the Kingdom realm. As you do, the dawning of the Kingdom realm of consciousness will become brighter and brighter. As the renewed mind becomes the predominant mind in which you live, focus your attention on your spirit and quietly await revelation. Like a student quietly awaiting the entrance of the teacher, so is the renewed mind quietly awaiting the appearance of the King in His Kingdom within.

Three: Stilling Your Emotions

While you are engaged in the exercise of stilling your mind and actively seeking Christ in His Kingdom, add another discipline—stilling your emotions. This discipline requires you to cast all your cares upon the Lord, for He cares for you. If you are prone to stress and worry, it would be best initially for you to engage in the discipline of practicing His Kingdom presence in the morning and evenings. These are generally the most restful times of the day for your mind and body. In the shower may be another good place. I find the sauna to be my favorite place to encounter the Lord. Finding places and certain times of the day where your emotions are quieter than others is important to help you experience greater success in stilling your emotions. The accomplishment of a goal increases our desire for more and ignites the Will to continue. Your emotions need to become subjected and enslaved to your Will. As you encounter unhealthy emotions, let your spirit's Will rise up as master, and gently calm them. If that doesn't work, stand strong, commanding your Will's desire. This requires engaging your thoughts and directing them onto your emotions. Imagine your thoughts being "you" and your "emotions" being a student in your classroom who needs to be quiet. If they don't listen the first time, "raise your voice." Your thoughts are the teacher; your emotions are willing students waiting for your direction. Your emotions are lousy masters but welcoming servants.

Authors Note: Emotions are a favorite stomping ground for the Devil. Overcoming his schemes requires your emotions coming under subjection to your spirit's Will. In the same way, a family requires leadership structure, so too does the human body. Learning to quiet emotions also requires an elevation of faith in Christ's ability to care for you. Getting your mind off earthly things and setting it on things above is a step in the direction of trusting the Lord. Meditate on the Kingdom. Study the attributes of your King and His Kingdom: His ability to care for you, His benevolence towards you. Learn about the economic system of the Lord. It rests upon His ownership of everything and His benevolent heart, providing you with all your needs according to His riches as you seek first His Kingdom. The more time you devote to seeking first the Kingdom, the less stress and anxiety you will experience. Paul shares a wonderful example of the fruit of seeking first the Kingdom when he said, *"I know what it is to be in need, and I know what it is to have plenty. I have learned the secret of being content in any and every situation, whether well fed or hungry, whether living in plenty or in want"* (Phil.4:12). Paul, through the understanding of the Lordship of Jesus, lived a life of quieted emotions as he became rooted in knowing the Father as his ultimate provider and source. Job is another example of an established Kingdom mindset: *"Naked I came from my mother's womb, and naked I will depart. The LORD gave, and the LORD has taken away; may the name of the LORD be praised."* (Job 1:21). Your emotions were never meant to experience anything but what ignites them from the Kingdom realm. There is a place where no external stimuli not originating from Heaven can adversely affect your emotions. Intrusive thoughts –those thoughts that originate outside yourself– may attempt to wreak havoc on them, but your discernment will quickly thwart the attempts. Circumstances may tempt you to worry and situations may test you with anxious feelings but those who carry the revelation of the Lordship of Jesus will rest safety in the storms of life. For an in depth understanding of Jesus' Lordship I recommend my book, *Discovering the Kingdom; A Guide to Seeking First the Kingdom*, especially chapters 8 and 9.

Most Americans suffer from stress and anxiety that makes the discipline of stilling emotions difficult. Furthermore, Satan uses "the cares of this world" as a major distraction not only in our pursuit of the Kingdom but our pursuit of the King as well. Nevertheless, make every effort to learn and master the craft of quieting your emotions. The greater your understanding of the Kingdom, the less anything is able to shake you. Exercise daily and often the discipline of stilling your emotions. Get in touch with your emotions. Examine regularly your emotional state and make corrections when imbalances are identified. I pray the Lord Jesus entice you into greater pursuit of stilling your emotions by giving you experiences with Him—experiences that captivate your attention, increase your faith, and produce a hunger and thirst for lengthier stillness. I also pray you educate yourself in the Lord's absolute sufficiency in His ability and desire to provide your every need, while granting you wisdom in discerning needs from wants.

Author's Note: My wife and I own a psychological clinic where we've found the supplement magnesium to be an effective tool in reducing stress and anxiety in the body. For those who suffer from heightened and out of balance emotional states, consider taking this. Although I am not a doctor, I would recommend taking higher amounts initially such as doubling the dosage recommendation on the bottle. Magnesium citrate or magnesium chelate are two of the best forms in my opinion. Other supplements that might aid in lowering stress and anxiety are adaptogen herbs such as Ashwagandha. We have found in severe cases, the sedative herb Valerian root or Lavender may be helpful. Use the recommended dosage for these herbs. It is the author's intention to have a sequel to this book dealing in depth with keys to optimizing the health of the body for the Lord's purposes. In this day and age, we cannot afford to underestimate the need to restore the temple–our bodies. The human body has become a malnourished dumping ground for toxic elements desperately needing restoration. The Lord is looking for cleansed temples in order to display His influence and splendor.

Four: Disengaging from Your Will

"For my thoughts are not your thoughts, neither are your ways my ways," declares the LORD."

Isaiah 55:8

I briefly mentioned that the soul is made up of your mind, will, and emotions. The step of disconnecting from your Will begins by recognizing your Will is not God's Will. Our Will, until it is brought under the rulership of the spirit, is self-centered, self-serving, and has in mind selfish ambition and emotional gratification. Without first disconnecting from your Will, you end up no different from the children of Israel who created God in their own image when they made the golden calf. Conversely, when we successfully disconnect from our Wills, which is a daily discipline, we make room for God's Will to take up active residence within us. This is not an easy task and one that will surely produce a war within—namely that of your flesh against the Spirit (Galatians 5:17). Stand strong and be patient. As the Lord separates your soul and spirit, you will find increased strength to overcome the desires of your Will through the reigning of your spirit man over your soul.

"For it is God who works in you to will and to act in order to fulfill his good purpose."

Philippians 2:13

Examine your desires and motives often. Line them up with what you understand to be the Lord's Will. Become familiar with what your Will is desiring. Repent when you realize it's not the Lord's. Agree with Him when your Will does not line up with His and be prepared to receive His unconditional love and forgiveness. Ask Him to transform your Will into the likeness of His. The redemptive plan of God includes the whole man—spirit, soul, and body. Don't limit His ability to conform you into His image. Christ lives in you; let Him be the hope of change. Actively engage your faith toward actualizing the reality that "I have been crucified with Christ." This requires deep work in us. The longer you remain in communion with Christ, the more your Will becomes familiar with His. This creates space for both Wills to enter oneness.

Author's Note: One practice that's helped me to disconnect from my Will is "silent prayer." This practice, in part, involves going before the Lord in prayer with a stilled mind. As you remain silent, wait for Him to speak. Because the Lord is usually slow to speak, it requires long periods of silence. During these moments, the carnal man will rise up and present its Will to the Lord. As these moments occur, you get a glimpse of "your Will" in action. It is the author's experience that your Will rises up persistently until it begins moving under the rulership of your spirit man and your soul has been transformed with adequate revelation of the Kingdom. A key to sustained periods of silent prayer is connecting with and enjoying the presence of the Lord.

Once you have obtained a somewhat mastery level of the above-mentioned disciplines, it is safe to assume your spirit man is well on its way to establishing dominion over your soul and body. This was God's original intent and a necessary work in demonstrating the Kingdom both within and on earth. We are no more capable of representing Christ and His Kingdom without this transformational process as a resurrected body is without first dying. God chose to dwell in man. The "holy of holies," the place of His dwelling within man, is our spirit. Subjecting our mind, Will, emotions, and body to our spirit is the same as subjecting our "self" to the Lord. This empowers the believer to live in a state of surrender with the Kings domain being flushed out in unison with us as we co-labor in union with Him, Spirit to spirit.

My greatest desire for you, dear reader is not that you experience the Lord's presence, although I'm sure you will. It's not that you take on the disciplines mentioned in this chapter to a mastery level. My greatest desire for you is that you enter into union with Christ in His Kingdom, through which you come to understand and experience His unconditional love. This union will be facilitated by the above-mentioned disciplines, but keep in mind; they are a means to an end, not the end itself. These disciplines are the means of bringing you into an abiding, intimate fellowship in the Spirit whereby unbroken communion with Christ, in His Kingdom within, is the goal. Keep your intentions of experiencing Christ in His Kingdom, not mastering disciplines. Seek first Christ and His Kingdom within. Use the disciplines; don't pursue the disciplines. As you put into practice these principles, I pray that your practice of His presence goes from minutes to hours, and from hours to days. It is then that we can anticipate the rule and reign of Christ on earth, through man, as He intended. With the birth of this new age of Kingdom consciousness, the Lord rules and reigns once again in His temple, displaying His glory and splendor to all things living.

> *"Now having been questioned by the Pharisees as to when the kingdom of God was coming, He answered them and said, "The kingdom of God is not coming with signs to be observed; nor will they say, 'Look, here it is!' or 'There it is!' For behold, the kingdom of God is within."*
> Luke 17:20-21

Like I said earlier, as long as we believe the external world is more impactful and real than the internal world, we will be stuck in this world's system. As soon as we catch the revelation that in fact, the internal world is far superior in every way to the external world, then we are given opportunity to enter the realm of existence we were created for, the realm of the Kingdom within! As we begin to incorporate these principles and endeavor to experience Christ, be mindful of our senses desire to receive the presence of the Lord for selfish gain. Remember, all that we do in this life is for the Lord. As we offer our lives a living sacrifice, know that we will need to lay on the alter our addiction to feeling good. There is nothing more satisfying and addicting than the Lords presence, but while we certainly are permitted to enjoy God, we want to enter into balance. We need to find the balance between enjoying His presence and being about the Fathers business of allowing Him to crucify our flesh and prepare us for His purposes.

CHAPTER 5

Walking in Resurrection Life through the Cross

There is a field of consciousness where the essence in creation comes alive and never before seen beauty in your fellow man is realized. A place where suffering meets a companion called peace and pain is eclipsed with hope. There are states of being within this field where the invisible becomes visible. Where good and bad disappear and are replaced with a life that awakens joy and peace deep within your soul. There is an invitation of ascension resonating in the human heart. A summons to transcend your present perceptual field. Conforming your mind to the patterns of Kingdom consciousness is the vehicle of transcendence. Carrying your cross and becoming clothed in the crucified life is the key to remaining in this Kingdom realm.

The resurrected life flowing through us is the life of Christ in us. The process of Christ's life flowing through us is predominantly reliant upon the carnal nature dying. To be crucified with Christ is to be joined with Him in the co-laboring effects of the Will of the Father on earth. The purpose of this chapter is to present insight, encouragement, and empowerment towards the crucified life with the end goal of seeing Christ in you expressed through you.

As I was in the spirit, I was caught up in a wind and realized it had carried me into a room. A door opened into my soul, and I saw the Lord standing on a threshing floor. On it was millions of crucibles. I could see through them even though they were solid. In the crucible, I saw Satan and his evil spirits. They were the fire in the crucible. Different groups of Saints were in the crucibles. Each crucible represented the degree to which the Saint's embraced the fire as the Lords hand of testing and refining. They were paying no attention to the evil and had accepted Satan and his company, not as an enemy but as a tool used for purification. I knew this to be a very important room for establishing Kingdom law on earth. For no Saint could be used to establish Kingdom law without the cleansing of fire. A deep cleansing is needed to become co-creators of Kingdom law on earth.

I began seeing multitudes of Saints not in the crucibles and became grieved. They refused to enter and were not being purified. A voice spoke, "Keep your eyes off everything but your assignment. Don't be distracted. Seek first the Kingdom of God and His righteousness. Seek only to do what you see the Lord doing. Deny yourself and pick up your cross daily."

The realities discovered while seeking first the Kingdom require humility and brokenness in order to be received properly. If we begin seeking first the Kingdom in the absence of intimate companionship with suffering and self-denial, we are in great danger of using Kingdom principles to build our own kingdom. This chapter is designed to provide you with the energy and empowerment for greater willingness to enter companionship with suffering. In this chapter, I introduce keys to remaining under burdens and receiving and even embracing circumstances which bring hurt and suffering. As you read, receive this chapter as an invitation not to suffer, but rather to have the blessings held within suffering made available to you when you are suffering. The goal of suffering is not to suffer, but to receive the unsearchable riches held in suffering, made available to all who embrace the cross for the sake of obedience to their King. Suffering presents numerous riches waiting to be revealed, the greatest of which is an attribute of Christ reserved exclusively for those suffering for His sake. May the fellowship with Christ found in suffering be yours. May the embrace of the cross empower you to enter the *"come up here"* realm, where you discover your "new creation" identity. An identity that empowers you to endure the cross as the eyes of your understanding become fixed on the joy that's set before you. Finding rest in the tension between our outer man perishing and our inner man being renewed is a key to abiding in resurrection life lived out of the realm of Kingdom consciousness.

"Pride goes before destruction, a haughty spirit before a fall."

Proverbs 16:18

Keys to the Kingdom

"Very truly I tell you, unless a kernel of wheat falls to the ground and dies, it remains only a single seed. But if it dies, it produces many seeds."
John 12:24

In March of 2005, I traveled to Mexico with a team from Wisconsin. We were attending an annual conference put on by one of the overseers of a Church I was ordained a teaching Elder. There were 17 nations represented and about 1500 people in attendance. Midway through the three-day event, I received a word for the nation of Mexico. I went to our overseer, told him, and he sent me to the platform where a man greeted me. He asked me to explain the word and I did. Immediately, he ushered me up the stairs, gave me a microphone, and told me to wait for him to signal me to share. About two minutes later the signal came, I shared the word, and the people erupted in praise.

I gave the microphone back to the stage director and re-entered the crowd of attendees. At the end of the evening, I was asked to share a meal with one of the leaders of an "apostolic" network expanding across Mexico. While conversing during the meal, he interrupted me and said, "Michael, you are a volcano about to erupt!" He shared several other encouraging words, we finished our evening, and I returned to my hotel. I spent the remainder of the evening in contemplation. While lying on my bed, I began dreaming of a big ministry impacting lots of people. I envisioned myself leading a team that would set Wisconsin on fire with a revival sure to sweep the region. My imagination grew larger and larger. After all, I had become the talk of the evening. My word set the conference and the Mexican people ablaze with hope. I had the approval and applause of our overseer, two established "apostles" over Mexico and the entire leadership team from Wisconsin.

By the time I landed in Wisconsin, I had the next year planned. I launched a ministry, established a board of directors, and began gathering other ministry leaders I felt would contribute to the fresh wave of revival I was certain was coming. By June, I had assembled about twenty leaders and began strategizing. We met at my home in a roundtable-like atmosphere. We all had our notebooks and were eager to share. I was energized and motivated to bring God's Kingdom to Wisconsin. My plan was materializing better than I had imagined. I felt like Wisconsin was on the launching pad of revival. The leaders were seasoned, I was on fire, and certain God was with me!

By August, I had verbal commitments from two big names in the faith to headline a conference I was putting together. My ministry was gaining momentum monthly, as the phone began ringing and speaking invitations were coming in. In the midst of all this apparent success, my foundation was being built on sand. My desire to do good was being rivaled by my fleshly desire to be elevated. The mixture was keeping me from building God's Kingdom. Part of me was building my own kingdom unawares. By September, my world collapsed with such force it destroyed everything I had built almost immediately. Virtually overnight, my life was turned upside down. I lost my wife, kids, ministry, home, friends, and was left with almost nothing. This didn't happen because of any secret sin or terrible actions on my part. When I look back, it was the grace of God allowing the Devil to sift me like wheat. My pride and the activity of building my own kingdom had put me in opposition to God. The Devil saw an opportune time to attempt to steal, kill, and destroy me. I had, through pride, been handed over to Satan with permission to be sifted like wheat.

The set of circumstances that would enter my world over the next ten years would be categorized by anyone as the worst of times. However, looking back they were the most important days of my life. They were both the worst of times and the best of times. I learned more about what it takes to become a disciple of Jesus during those difficult years than in any other time in my life. If a dream does not die a thousand deaths, it will likely become building material for a kingdom other than the Lord's. Unless a dream falls into the ground and dies, it remains by itself. But if it dies, it will give birth too much lasting fruit.

The greatest lesson was that of denying myself, picking up my cross and following Jesus. This discipline was presented to me in an exaggerated and extended manner for years. Life's circumstances were painful, and I often failed in my surrendering to the "dying of self" that was taking place. I was abandoned by almost every important person in my life at the time leaving me with only one relationship—Jesus. During this time, I began discovering the cost of following Him. I was presented with opportunities I thought were curses from the Devil—only to find out they were meant for my good. For example, when my kids were taken from me briefly, I was devastated. During this time, however, the Lord showed me how I had stronger affection and love for them than I did for Him. I don't know if I would have come to this realization any other way. As a follower of Jesus, with the desire to be a disciple, I learned I needed to have that corrected. The Lord showed me my error by opening the scripture that reads, *"If anyone comes to me and does not hate father and mother, wife and children, brothers and sisters—yes, even their own life—such a person cannot be my disciple"* (Luke 14:26). It took separation from my children, for God to show me my need for realignment of relational priorities. Once I saw this, I repented and over time was reunited with my kids. Only this time, by the power of the Holy Spirit, my love and affections were properly aligned. Today, I'm enjoying a healthy, balanced relationship with all four of my kids.

The ambition that was driving and motivating my desire for ministry also needed to be exposed. Because selfish ambition was part of what was driving me, I was clearly building my own kingdom, despite my love and adoration for the Lord. I was immature, naive, and blinded too many snares of the enemy which, if permitted, would have brought reproach to the Kingdom of God and produced a glaring misrepresentation of the Lord and His Church. I needed to die to myself. My Will, desires, ambition, and pursuits needed to come to an end and in God's great mercy, He allowed Satan to sift many of those unhealthy attributes from me. I was placed in a position where I had two choices: become bitter, resentful, and angry or trust God in the midst of the darkest period of my life.

Sometime during the initial months of this "kernel of wheat falling into the ground and dying" season, I remembered a book I read about six months before my world collapsed. The title is *Crucified by Christians.* It was a book that chronicled the journey of a believer and the pain he goes through. At the end of the book, author Gene Edwards reveals it was the Father who allowed all the hurt and pain. And the purpose? To crucify our flesh in order that we may enter a resurrected life. Recalling the book brought such comfort I picked it up and reread it. To this day, it was the most impactful book I have ever read. Such a deep revelation of the necessity of dying daily was etched into my soul. This revelation has empowered me to pick up my cross and is disciplining me to die to the self-life that consistently wants to rise up and take control. The longer you cling to your cross, the less your self-life arises. The greater your understanding of the need to carry your cross, the more effective you become in carrying it.

Reading *Crucified by Christians* a second time impacted me as much or more than the first. Knowing the Father was allowing every painful event in my life somehow diminished the pain and freed me to forgive. Despite the enormous injustice I accrued, the arrows of anger, resentment, bitterness, and revenge were strangely absent. I began looking at my pain in a different light. Instead of seeing it as mistreatment and injustice, I began perceiving it as an instrument of death for the purpose of crucifixion. I began to see a bigger picture. I began seeing pain and injustice from a larger perspective. I learned all cross bearing experiences are designed to bring you to the crucifixion. I discovered the crucifixion was created as an instrument of death and death was the pathway to resurrection life in the realm of the Kingdom. My entire way of thinking began shifting, and a whole new reality emerged before my eyes.

Ironically, this change of mind did not diminish the pain and sorrow of my circumstances. It did, however, empower me through the suffering process. There is a substance found in pain and suffering that once discovered, propels you to endure with greater fortitude. This substance is none other than the Lord Jesus revealing a part of His nature reserved for those suffering for His sake. The awareness that I was fellowshipping with Him in my suffering brought to me an expectancy that was waking up the divine nature in me while simultaneously killing the life of my carnal nature. With the understanding that the Father holds all circumstances in his hand, brings empowerment to make it through even the greatest of garden of Gethsemane experiences. There is a joy in the journey to the resurrected life. This joy overshadows all circumstances and takes you to a place where you hear Jesus declare over you, *"My grace is sufficient for you, for my power is made perfect in weakness."* Your response? *"Therefore I will boast all the more gladly about my weaknesses, so that Christ's power may rest on me."* (2Corinthians 12:9). *"I die every day"* Paul said in 1 Corinthians 15:31.

As representatives of the Kingdom of Heaven on earth, we are called to live life from the realm of Heaven on earth. We are in the world, but not of the world. We live on earth, but our life is experienced from a seated position in Heaven and expressed out of the realm of Heaven on earth. Only resurrected bodies are found in Heaven, therefore it is necessary we die daily. This ensures our abode remains in Heaven. This is not a religious activity we do, but rather a daily decision we make, trusting the cross to perform its work. We are no more capable of killing our carnal nature than man alone is capable of righteousness. To die daily is to yield ourselves over to the work of the cross, accepting whatever comes our way as an instrument in the Lord's hand meant for our good. It is intended to conform us into His image through the death and resurrection of our faculties. If we define the cross as any circumstance we find that rubs us the wrong way, then we can be assured of numerous attempts throughout every day to carry our cross. This presents us many opportunities daily of surrendering our Will over in quiet submission, just like a sheep is led to the slaughter (See Isaiah 53:7).

Author's Note: Picking up our cross daily grows into dying daily to everything outside the Will and purposes of the Father. There is however one aspect of the dying process that I believe is most important and impactful and it deals with the mind. When Jesus said to seek first the Kingdom He was, in effect, asking us to crucify the aspect of our lives that deals with the information we choose to receive. He was asking us to make it our top priority to receive the message of the gospel of the Kingdom–the information of the Kingdom above all other forms and fields of information. This, in my experience, is the most transformational decision a human can make in choosing the crucified life. We are conditioned to receive all sorts of information, most of it either feeds our flesh or carnal mind. Seeking first the Kingdom, however, builds up our inner man, feeds the life of Christ in us, and grows the renewed mind which is consciousness in the Kingdom. If you are hesitant about committing to the crucified life, I encourage you to at least give seeking first the information of the Kingdom a try. Commit to less time engaged in entertainment and idol conversation. Commit to changing your thought life so as to fill it with more time pondering the Kingdom. Start by laying down one or two activities that serve no eternal purpose, and in exchange, take that time to seek the Kingdom.

> *"I have been crucified with Christ and I no longer live, but Christ lives in me. The life I now live in the body, I live by faith in the Son of God, who loved me and gave himself for me."*
>
> Galatians 2:20)

Paul, through years of surrender to the Lordship of Christ, was given insight into a mystery with such profound implications only those dead to themselves are privileged to see and experience. The revelation that Jesus controls everything in our lives makes way for us to lay down our perceived need to control life's circumstances. The more we consciously lay down control, the more revelation of the Lordship of Jesus we receive. This revelation perpetuates and stimulates a desire in us to die to our ways. In God's sovereign time, He reveals Christ in us. The longer we remain in a posture of desiring His Will over ours, the more the life of Christ in us arises. The greater our awareness of suffering being a doorway that opens to us the treasure hidden in us, the greater the experience of the power of God flowing through us.

No longer living from the carnal nature requires being in conscious contact with our conscience—the part of our nature that reveals to us whether we are living through "Christ in me" or from our carnal nature. As we cultivate humility and rely upon Holy Spirit to empower us in the death of self, we are given insight into which nature is working in us at any given moment. The key is clothing ourselves in humility and acquiring the discipline of awareness of conscience. As awareness of our conscience reaches maturity it moves to our subconscious and morphs into discernment, becoming part of the fabric of our nature. Don't become overwhelmed at your carnal nature's desire to remain alive. God isn't. He is so aware of it that He sent Christ to live in you, knowing you needed a conquering agent to overcome your self-life. Not only does He forgive all your past sins, but all future sins have been placed under the cleansing and forgiving blood of Jesus. Settle, once and for all, that your God loves you unconditionally. Understanding this frees you to avail your self-life more readily which gives opportunity for Christ to show Himself strong on your behalf. Additionally, posturing your heart in humble surrender quickens the life of Christ in you, drawing your Will toward the divine nature. The more we become aware of Christ in us and His activity, the more we are changed.

> *"But we all, with open face beholding as in a glass the glory of the Lord, are changed into the same image from glory to glory, even as by the Spirit of the Lord."*
>
> 2 Cor. 3:18

In my first book, *Discovering the Kingdom*, I present a list of criteria for becoming a disciple. I put together the list after reading the New Testament and identifying what Jesus revealed to be necessary qualifications to entering the identity of a disciple and expressing substance reserved for those walking in the identity of one. I list 16 scriptural characteristics. All of them imply, to one degree or another, both explicitly and implicitly, the need to suffer. For example, a disciple is required to deny themselves, pick up their cross, give up everything, and lay down their own Will. They're also told they will endure great persecution. Here, Jesus makes clear the cost of receiving the secrets of the Kingdom—which is what a disciple receives. The other criteria for discipleship are less explicit about our need to suffer, but the fact of suffering is evident. I share this with you in the hope that the next time you become mindful of suffering, instead of focusing on the pain, you shift your thinking to the reason—in order to prepare you for the proper handling of the secrets of the Kingdom. Remember, the pain is inflicted on your outer man for the purpose of killing him, but the death blows to your outer man are simultaneously renewing your inner man. Accept and even embrace the pain but place your attention and thanksgiving on your inner man's renewal.

In 1994, I started my first business. Almost immediately, I began making lots of money. Checks were coming in from clients that were larger than I'd ever seen. Greed began surfacing in my heart. I began desiring a nicer car, fancier clothes and was preoccupied with buying my first home. This self-centered thought life scared me. I made a decision that I would no longer keep track of my income. Instead, each month I would deposit the checks, pay my bills, and any leftover money would go toward school loans. Within one year, $55,000.00 in school loans and all remaining debt was paid off. It was about that time the Lord spoke to me, "I want you to begin keeping track of your income." My initial thought was "I rebuke you, Devil. That only causes my carnal nature to rise up." The Lord responded, "Michael, I know that nature is in you. I don't want you to suppress it; I want it to rise up. Suppressing it keeps it alive in you. Allowing it to rise up gives me permission to kill it as long as that is your desire." This paradigm shift allowed me to begin looking at my finances. Sure enough, my carnal, self-centered nature rose up consistently. Through years of confession and repentance, the Lord eventually crucified the life of my carnal nature toward money. Today, through the life of Christ in me, I have been given His perspective toward money. This grew a confident trust in His ability to provide for me as well as a healthy perspective of "things."

Don't suppress your carnal nature; rather, be authentic before the Lord. As the carnal self-life presents itself, acknowledge it, and ask the Lord to crucify it. Make a decision to pick up your cross in the area of self-life being exposed and trust the Lord to work a divine exchange—

His life for yours. As circumstances come into your life that rubs you the wrong way, acknowledge them as being agents of crucifixion. The more we connect unwanted events to instruments of crucifixion, the faster the transformation occurs. He who has begun the work in you will be faithful to complete it!

> *"Very truly I tell you, unless a kernel of wheat falls to the ground and dies, it remains only a single seed. But if it dies, it produces many seeds."*
>
> John 12:24

> *"The field is the world; the good seed is the children of the kingdom, but the tares are the children of the wicked one."*
>
> Matthew 13:38

A seed contains the whole of its kind. An apple seed contains the entire apple tree. Not until the apple seed dies, does it make room for the apple tree. In the same manner, a human being contains the Kingdom—so to must we die before the Kingdom comes forth. The human is the "seed." When we die, it brings forth the essence of who we are—the Kingdom. The appearance of an acorn is that of a light brown, round-like object roughly the size of an olive. The essence of the acorn, however, is an oak tree. In order for the essence to express itself, the acorn must die. The invisible nature of the acorn is only made visible through the process of death. When Jesus declared, "I confer upon you a Kingdom" and *"the Kingdom of God is within you"* He was identifying you as a seed. As we "put to death the old nature," the Kingdom is brought forth—first in our field of consciousness, then onto the earth. In order for the invisible qualities of the Kingdom to be made visible, we must enter the process of death modeled by our beloved friend and leader, Jesus.

Man's appearance and essence are very different. Our appearance is made up of all things within our carnal nature. Our essence is the Kingdom within us, for the Kingdom of God is within. This Kingdom appears only as we die to self. The decision to disconnect from the desires of the flesh gives way to the opening of a new life given to us at the new birth. God wants *"Christ in us"* to become the essence of all areas of our lives. This is a lifelong process that begins with a commitment to deny ourselves and pick up our cross of self-denial.

The cross is designed as an instrument of pain and suffering only so long as we lack revelation of its purpose—awakening the essence of who we are through the resurrected life. As we gain greater perspective of this resurrected life, the cross becomes an embraceable instrument we desperately need and even long for. The more we pursue the resurrected life, the more we realize the necessity of the crucified life. Paul, in Romans 7, expressed his longing to have his carnal nature die. He came to the appreciation that his identity was no longer in his carnal man. Through revelation, by the grace of God, he saw himself in Christ. As he poured out his heart to the Lord, we see how the spirit of Wisdom showed him both natures at work in him. Look at his longing to have his true nature, the Kingdom, and the Christ-life expressed. Paul received this revelatory privilege in part because he was given the grace to implement the means—dying to self while knowing Christ in Him would not only save him from himself but become the life in which he would find his true being in. We live and move and have our being either in our carnal nature or the divine nature. Carrying our cross becomes the soil in which the divine nature sprouts. Read this:

"We know that the law is spiritual, but I am unspiritual, sold as a slave to sin. I do not understand what I do. For what I want to do I do not do, but what I hate I do. And if I do what I do not want to do, I agree that the law is good. As it is, it is no longer I myself who do it, but it is sin living in me. For I know that good itself does not dwell in me, that is, in my sinful nature. For I have the desire to do what is good, but I cannot carry it out. For I do not do the good I want to do, but the evil I do not want to do—this I keep on doing. Now if I do what I do not want to do, it is no longer I who do it, but it is sin living in me that does it. So I find this law at work: Although I want to do good, evil is right there with me. For in my inner being I delight in God's law; but I see another law at work in me, waging war against the law of my mind and making me a prisoner of the law of sin at work within me. What a wretched man I am! Who will rescue me from this body that is subject to death? Thanks be to God, who delivers me through Jesus Christ our Lord!

Romans 7:14-25

In the same way, the divine nature comes from Christ and Christ alone, so too does deliverance. If you began in the Spirit, don't try to perfect in the flesh only what can be accomplished in the Spirit. It is and always will be Christ that begins and finishes the work. Understanding of this truth takes you to the place where a life of rest and confident trust awaits you. Open yourself up to the bountiful mercy and endless love of the Lord. Become an antenna, receiving from Heaven, and you will discover the Heart of the Father—a heart full of all that you long for and all that you need—in ever-deepening ways.

> *"For the joy set before him, he endured the cross, scorning its shame, and sat down at the right hand of the throne of God."*
> Hebrews 12:2

Vision of our future is an important catalyst into the purposes of God for our lives. In order to enter our place of rest, ruling and reigning on earth from the Kingdom realm of consciousness, we must receive sight into our future. Vision enables us to effectively carry our cross knowing where it leads us. There is an empowering of life in the present when we receive and hold onto vision of our future. We remain in the present, but have adequate awareness of our future in our peripheral. All good coaches present their teams with a vision of winning a championship. Throughout the season the team is reminded of it often. The coaches purpose, in part, is to give incentive during times when they are being worked extra hard. This vision of winning a championship serves as an energizer, giving strength to persevere through the difficult times. The Lord is no different toward us. Joel prophesied that in the last days,:

> *"I will pour out my Spirit on all people. Your sons and daughters will prophesy, your old men will dream dreams, your young men will see visions."*
> Joel 2:28

During difficult periods in life, bring to your remembrance the dreams, visions, and prophesies over your life. As these visions are drawn up in your heart, let them become strength to you. Allow the awareness of these dreams and desires to empower you through heavy cross bearing seasons. Use your imagination to dream with God. Find friends and family to encourage you. Don't hesitate to seek encouragement in times of struggle. If you have no one to lean on, run to the Lord, an ever-present help in time of need. As you put into practice this principle, anticipate and watch strength mount up within you. Keep in mind that all prophetic words are spoken to your spiritual man, but your carnal man must first die in order for the word to come alive. Be of good cheer, you are one death closer to the Word coming alive through you.

> *"Even though Jesus was God's Son, he learned obedience from the things he suffered."*
> Hebrews 5:8

How did Jesus learn obedience from the things he suffered? If suffering itself produces obedience, then how come I'm not much more obedient than I am? Jesus learned obedience from the things He suffered because He understood the purpose of suffering—to bring Him into obedience. Not only so but He became willing to accept suffering as a means to this end. Instead of rebuking unwanted circumstances, He Willfully accepted and even embraced them at times. No matter if it was a minor nuisance or a life-threatening experience, His full faith and trust were in His Father. To embrace suffering as a means to obedience is to follow Christ which places you under the All-Powerful hand of the King of kings. Additionally, it opens access to experiencing the environment in which you live—the place the Bible calls "in Christ."

The way in which we perceive suffering determines how it affects us. When suffering is viewed as coming from the enemy, we invite the enemy to use it for his purposes. When we enter into "battle," anger, frustration, and resentment often result. We become weary. We strive and labor to distance ourselves from the suffering only to realize we are laboring in the flesh—keeping our carnal nature alive and in control. Viewing suffering as a tool that forms obedience and conforms us into the image of Christ, gives rise to a view from a heavenly perspective. Further understanding that the circumstances causing the suffering are not allowed without the permissive Will of our loving Father empowers us to allow the suffering to serve us more effectively. Cultivate a heavenly perspective on suffering, and you will catch the wind of the Spirit and begin soaring with the eagles.

> *"For the message of the cross is foolishness to those who are perishing, but to us who are being saved, it is the power of God."*
> 1 Corinthians 1:18

In the Kingdom, resurrected life is the result of death. It's not possible for the Lord to awaken the Kingdom realm of consciousness within us, without first conditioning us to carry our cross by denying our self-life. The Biblical narrative leading to the death and resurrection of Jesus contains keys to the power of God. Keys that Paul told us would be found in the "message of the cross." The "message of the cross" Paul was referring to was not merely that of Jesus dying on the cross. As important as that was, there is a present-day message, a new covenant message of the cross that will unleash the power of God against the powers and principalities presently enslaving Nations. Both messages are vital. One is to be accepted and appreciated in our minds, and the other lived out and experienced in our personal, daily lives.

> *"Then he said to them all: "Whoever wants to be my disciple must deny themselves and take up their cross daily and follow me."*
> Luke 9:23 NIV

The message of the cross is an invitation to followers of Jesus to walk not only in His footsteps but in His Will. It's an invitation to become vulnerable, transparent, and willing to live life thinking less of ourselves. The cross' invitation is not for you to change, but rather become willing to be changed. Apart from Him, we can do nothing. Keep in mind; it is God that works in you both to Will and to do His good pleasure. This willingness opens the door for the Lord to begin reprogramming and reforming you away from the pattern of this world and into the image of Himself. To the degree we see the depths of our own depravity and the beauty of a resurrected life is the degree we will surrender our Wills and take up our cross. Our responsibility is to make a decision to deny ourselves what we want in exchange for another life—the life of Christ in us.

In a practical sense, the denying of ourselves is the pathway to experiencing the life of Christ in us. The more we are able to break down our self-life, the more Christ in us appears to our conscious experience. Fasting is an effective tool used to break down the self-life. Anytime we starve our bodies, emotions, senses and all other parts of "self," we make room for the Lord to appear to us in more tangible ways.

There are three kingdoms presently operating on the earth: the kingdom of darkness, the Kingdom of light, and the kingdom of man within us. The ruler of the kingdom within man is our Will. Both the Kingdom of darkness and the Kingdom of light want control of man's Will. The Will of man is yoked to one kingdom or another at all times. The Kingdom of light's instrument of gaining control of our Will is through repentance and the cross. The moment you make a decision to pick up your cross, you enter into a relationship with the Kingdom of light that sets you on the road to resurrected life. The kingdom of darkness doesn't simply surrender in defeat. It has its own agenda and will work to disconnect you from your engagement with the Kingdom of light. The desire to satisfy your own Will is a testimony that your nature is still alive. This desire is where the kingdom of darkness moves its traps and attempts to fan the flames of these desires.

While the Will of man is the king of the carnal man, other aspects of a man's nature have occupied the throne. Emotions, for example, govern many of us. We are prone to respond to feelings unconsciously, often not even considering if they are rational or not. The moment we experience a feeling it takes over our senses, and we respond in kind with the emotion. We have been demoted to emotional creatures instead of God's created design for us as legal humans. Emotions play a vital role in fulfilling God's desire for us. They do, however, need to be placed back under the governance of our spirits. Emotions make wonderful servants, but slave drivers when placed in the role of a master.

Many people are controlled by their senses, particularly sight. Vision elicits an emotional response only produced as our sight connects with something. So many of us are addicted to TV because of the emotional responses produced by what we see and hear. Our emotions drive us into containment as we're entertained through the stimulation and arousal of our emotions. Most American entertainment drives us into a containment that feeds our carnal nature, ensuring the renewed mind never expresses the realm of Kingdom consciousness. Once again we have been conditioned so successfully that most are unaware of any of this. Awakening to these shortcomings is paramount to the process of dying to self. If we don't know what it is we need to die to, it makes it very difficult for our Wills to disengage from the carnal exercise. Furthermore, without knowing the sinful nature of our self-life, it becomes impossible to confess our sins—the spark that ignites the power of God to bring about cleansing. *"'If we confess our sins he is faithful ... to cleanse us ..."* (1 John 1:9).

Despite the Will of man being created to play a role in reigning with Christ in the human body, it too has suffered a mighty fall from its ordained position. It has become self-centered instead of Kingdom centered. It has chosen to build its own kingdom instead of becoming joint heirs in Christ's, allowing the Lord to lead and direct us in His affairs.

We need the death of our wayward, carnal self-life daily. We desperately need the remedy for our fallen and corrupt existence. The cross is God's solution to destroying man's waywardness while simultaneously bringing to life His divine nature. To the believer, carrying the cross becomes the eruption allowing the molten lava of God's inner Kingdom to flow out of us. Buried deep within man's carnal nature is resurrected life waiting to surface. The emergence is contingent upon the self-life's death.

A key to bearing the weight of the cross is focusing on the divine nature rising in you and not on the pain coming from the death of your carnal nature. Setting your attention on the presence of Christ in you diminishes the pain and empowers you to carry on. Understand, God is not wishing to kill you; He wants to resurrect you. This perspective is powerful. He wants to Kingdomize every fallen nature you have. He wants to set apart the members of your body for His purposes. In order to accomplish this, we must allow our Wills to line up with Christ's and govern our decisions long enough for the cross to have a great enough effect that we become strengthened and never turn back. When you experience pain from the cross, there are always two voices crying out. Your carnal nature is violently trying to get your attention, demanding you stop such foolishness. Its desire is to live life in an easier, more desirable way. The other voice, however, the still small voice of Christ in you, is waiting to empower you. He's anticipating giving of Himself to you in sweet fellowship. Sweet, sweet fellowship is only offered to the broken, hurting, cross-bearing follower of Christ.

> *"Therefore we do not lose heart. Though outwardly we are wasting away, yet inwardly we are being renewed day by day."*
>
> 2 Corinthians 4:16

A key to enduring the cross is distinguishing between your outer and inner man through the dividing of soul and spirit. Once we do, we are positioned to direct our attention on the renewing that's taking place in our inner man. Once we fix our eyes on the inner man, the pain being inflicted on the outer man subsides. Furthermore, understanding that the outer man is the fleshly, carnal, self-centered part of you, strengthens one's resolve to persevere all the way to the crucifixion.

Perseverance is another key to carrying your cross. In high school, my son ran cross country. I used to stand at the finish line admiring the runners' perseverance. One race it dawned on me, and I thought, "Perseverance elevates you to a position whereby overcoming the self-life is possible." There may be no greater and more effective way to deny yourself than persevering. Its very act requires you to deny present needs and desires in favor of something outside yourself—something greater. The greater your vision, the more likely you are to persevere. The more mindful you are about the purpose of self-denial, the greater the resurrection life will burst forth. The more you persevere, the longer you remain in a posture of denying yourself. The more you deny yourself, the easier it becomes for Christ to crown you with resurrection life.

Every part of your mind, Will, emotions, and body contains the essence of Christ's nature. A key to His nature bursting through you is your carnal nature dying.

> *"Unless a kernel of wheat first dies it remains a single seed. But if it dies He is enabled to burst forth!"* (paraphrase).
>
> John 12:24

As the different parts of your self-life die, they come under the Lordship of Christ. As He redeems them, He empowers you to respond and reflect His nature through your self-life which has become one with Christ. As your Will dies, it comes under the Lordship of Jesus, becoming one with His Will. He redeems your Will as He reveals His Will and empowers you to fulfill it. As you surrender your mind to the Lord and He begins sharing His with you, it opens a door for us to die to our thoughts. This revelation requires us to examine all activity in our life. In doing so, we realize how corrupt our carnal minds are and how much information we allow in that is contrary to His mind. As we die to self, we lay down activities we once thought were harmless. TV shows, entertainment, and other activities that once entertained us will be put away. Where and how we spend our time will suddenly change as we become aware of how detrimental things we presently desire are to the resurrected life.

When we were born again, Christ came and made His home in us. His desire is to come out of us and begin touching those we come in contact with. In order to do this, however, He must come through us. Before His nature and likeness are expressed, we must put to death our nature. Otherwise, when He comes out of us, His nature will be contaminated with ours and what we present will fall short of the image of Christ and His Kingdom. Freshwater cannot flow together with salt water. The contamination ruins its nature altogether. The flow of the Spirit must come through clean vessels. The cross is the means of providing the Spirit of Jesus access out of us in a pure and undefiled manner, presenting Himself to the world accurately and authentically.

No man can walk the Jesus way without a consistent punch in the face. Necessary is the help of a messenger of Satan.

> *"And lest I should be exalted above measure by the abundance of the revelations, a thorn in the flesh was given to me, a messenger of Satan to buffet me, lest I be exalted above measure. Concerning this thing, I pleaded with the Lord three times that it might depart from me. And He said to me, 'My grace is sufficient for you, for My strength is made perfect in weakness.' Therefore most gladly I will rather boast in my infirmities, that the power of Christ may rest upon me. Therefore I take pleasure in infirmities, in reproaches, in needs, in persecutions, in distresses, for Christ's sake. For when I am weak, then I am strong."*
> 2 Corinthians 12:7-10

What a remarkable discovery Paul had. He not only came to the realization that hardships were necessary, but was empowered to settle into the hardships pleasurably. He took delight and responded in full gladness at the privilege of suffering for Christ's sake. Paul learned that there is a purpose in suffering that propelled him to take pleasure in whatever circumstance he found himself in. The willingness to shift your mindset as it relates to hardships is necessary to the development of the grace of God—Divine empowerment—in your personal experience. The perceptual awareness to see all things working together for our good, in conjunction with the discipline to train our thoughts in this direction will awaken divine empowerment. The example Paul left for us is worthy of our attention. Beyond our attention, this example serves as an invitation to seek the place of contentment no matter the condition we find ourselves. This place of contentment rises in our consciousness as we understand a principle in Paul's phrase, *"For when I am weak, then I am strong."* The principle being, when you are weak, you are weak in your carnal nature. When you are strong, you are strong in your new nature which is Christ in you.

Paul's struggles came as a result of "the abundance of the revelations." The messenger of Satan came from the Lord to ensure the revelations would continue to flow to Paul for the purpose of the Kingdom's growth. As the Church enters the realm of the *"come up here,"* one of the attributes of a life in this realm is "the abundance of the revelations." Therefore, we must commit to a life filled with messengers of Satan buffeting us. The sooner you condition your mind to count it all joy whenever you encounter such opposition the broader your Kingdom travels will be and the greater the Kingdom mysteries are opened to you. Therefore, *"take pleasure in infirmities, in reproaches, in needs, in persecutions, in distresses, for Christ's sake."* (2 Corinthians 12:10a) **For when you are weak, then you are strong.**

Steps to Resurrected Life

Looking closely at Jesus' final day leading to His crucifixion, we discover keys to the resurrected life. Gleaning from the narrative, many call the Stations of the Cross, let's engage our Wills steadfastly toward the resurrection while keeping in mind the necessity of the cross. Let us consider our calling to die into a life of resurrection. Knowing the only bodies alive in Heaven are those of a resurrected nature, let us develop the discipline of daily carrying our cross, knowing it's Christ in us that empowers us in all we do. As we consider the Stations of the Cross, I pray we receive insight, revelation, comfort, and inspiration to follow in Jesus' footsteps. While drawing insight into what empowered and enabled Jesus to bear His cross, I pray these keys come alive in and through us. Keep in mind, it's the renewed mind that brings the appearance of the Kingdom realm of consciousness, but it's the cross that enables us to walk in the Kingdom realm. To live in the Kingdom, you must die daily.

First Station: Jesus is Condemned to Death

Jesus was first condemned to death by Pilot. However, we know it was not Pilot who held His fate, but Jesus. "I lay down my life on my own accord." What placed the cross on Jesus' back was no man, no demon, and no government ruler. It was His Will. Not only Jesus' Will but the steadfast devotion to His decision—a resolute and purposeful commitment to die. Even in the most difficult time of His life, the garden of Gethsemane, while tempted to divorce Himself from His commitment, He remained intentional and steadfast by exclaiming, *"Father, if it be possible to take this cup from me ... nevertheless not my will but your will be done."* Our Lord had such commitment to the Father's Will that even when He "disagreed" with it, He was able to remain connected to it. Jesus' deep, intimate, abiding relationship with His Father awakened in Him the realization of the superior nature of the Father's Will. Jesus had the awareness to recognize when His emotions threatened to take the throne within Him, to cling to His unchanging Father's Will until He was able to re-establish the Father's Will within Him. This discipline can only be experienced through the power of the Holy Spirit living in you and a deep understanding of the Father's Will.

An important question to answer and understand is this: who killed Jesus? Both answers are shocking but important to accept. It was Jesus' own people under the direction of the Father. Shocking, I know, but true. For further understanding into this truth, I direct you to Gene Edwards' book "Crucified by Christians." Understanding this difficult truth brings a removal of the sting of death and opens a space for us to enter deeper states of rest during suffering. A rest that joins us in spirit with Paul's experiential knowing that, *"Death has been swallowed up in victory."* (1 Corinthians 15:54b) Therefore, *"Where, O death, is your victory? Where, O death, is your sting?"* (1 Corinthians 15:55)

Most of us have been wounded and even crucified by our own family, friends, and those of the household of faith. In fact, they are the ones capable of hurting us since strangers have little influence over us. As we take a moment and consider how we've been hurt, let's take time to forgive. Use this opportunity to bring healing to yourself by letting go of any bitterness, resentment, anger, or ill-will. Ask the Lord to forgive you for holding those who hurt you in an unhealthy manner. Ask for personal healing while forgiving any wrongdoing. As you do, know you've just enacted healing through your decision. Don't let emotions rob you of your transformational act by tricking you into thinking nothing happened because you "feel" no different. Forgiveness is a decision, not a feeling. As you maintain conscious contact with your decision, reminding yourself you forgave, sooner or later your emotions will stop contradicting your forgiveness.

In the same manner, Christ laid His life down, let's be intentional to do likewise. Become willing to suffer for a higher cause. Accept persecution and hardships as not coming from the one inflicting the pain, but rather as a means of living the crucified life. Don't let anyone kill you, but rather choose to lay down your life. Condition your Will to align itself under the Will of the Father, esteeming His above yours. The resurrected life comes with a price. The initial costly expense is nothing compared to the riches that await all those who endure to the end! There are power and encouragement in knowing that the seed carrying resurrected life is the cross. Carrying your cross is the means to watering the seed which causes resurrection life to spring forth. Christ in you awaits the opportunity to become your resurrected life. He longs to once again become the change agent upon the earth, only this time laboring in you and through you. What an opportunity! What a privilege! What a God!

Second Station: Jesus Carries His Cross Third Station: Jesus Falls The First Time and Fifth Station: Simon of Cyrene Helps Jesus To Carry His Cross

Jesus' journey to resurrected life found Him falling under the weight of the cross. The One, who laid down His life as God, making Himself the son of man, needed help carrying His cross. This help came in the form of a man named Simon of Cyrene. To all who are carrying your cross, you can rest assured the Lord has a Simon of Cyrene waiting for you. When you think your cross has become too heavy to bear, know help is near. If you have no one, ask the Lord Himself to become your Simon of Cyrene. Draw near to Him, and He will draw near to you. Wait patiently on the Lord, and He will renew your strength. There is no one more familiar with what you're going through than He. There is also no one with more understanding of how important it is you learn to carry your own cross daily. Place yourself on the altar of His sovereignty and wait with patience. Use times of extraordinary pain as a trigger for you to set your gaze upon the future—a future full of resurrected life—a future full of joy and fulfillment. Remember, it was the joy set before our Lord that empowered Him to endure the cross. Encourage yourself by dreaming and imagining your future in the Lord. Dream big and use your imagination to soar above the pain that the cross produces. Remember, the cross is designed to bring death to your outer man but renewal to your inner man.

When carrying our cross, it becomes necessary to understand that we are, in and of ourselves, incapable of doing so. When the weight of the cross becomes overbearing, let the burden serve as a reminder of our need for divine empowerment. Use those times of overwhelming pain as a catalyst driving you to seek strength outside of your self-life. Discipline yourself to rely upon the Lord, a very present help in times of need. Condition your thought life to depart from the awareness of the pain, choosing to embrace vision, destiny, and the joy set before you. Fix your mind on things above. Search deeply for Christ in you, relying on Him and Him alone. Any cross you are capable of carrying yourself does not lead to resurrected life. Additionally, condition your way of thinking to direct attention toward searching for the Holy Spirit as your strength. As Simon of Cyrene became the strength Jesus needed to continue His journey to the crucifixion, so too is the Holy Spirit to become our strength. It requires a reconditioning in our thoughts in order to see Him as our ever-present help in times of need.

Forth Station: Jesus Meets His Mother

Meeting His mother, a type and shadow of the Holy Spirit, was no doubt a source of strength and comfort. Although it was a sobering and painful experience for Mary, Jesus likely saw her as a reminder of His purpose. One look into her eyes ignited a flame of desire to continue. Her voice entering His ear no doubt propelled Him with strength not present prior to this love connection. As you encounter the Holy Spirit in your journey to resurrected life, I trust you will be empowered and edified. He will place Himself before you at strategic times. When He does, be sure to connect with Him. Don't just pass Him by. Be mindful that as Jesus was strengthened by the presence of Mary, so too are we strengthened by the Holy Spirit. Keep in mind; the Holy Spirit is known as the Comforter because the Holy Spirit comforts. If you're not experiencing comfort, it may be the Lord is trying to teach you something. Since the Holy Spirit is also a teacher, posture yourself as a student and listen intently. He might want you to learn something before He presents Himself as Comforter.

Not only does strength come to us through the Holy Spirit but the opening of the Kingdom within. Because the Kingdom is in the Holy Spirit, our encounter with Him during this portion of our cross—bearing experience reveals the dawning of a new existence—the field of Kingdom consciousness emerging out from the budding of resurrection life. This resurrection life begins germinating throughout the dying process, providing us with strength to continue on the path leading to crucifixion.

Because the Kingdom is in the Holy Spirit, each revelation of the Holy Spirit is a revelation of the Kingdom. The essence of the Holy Spirit is the Kingdom. All that is within the Holy Spirit is the Kingdom. Therefore, as we continue carrying our cross, the Holy Spirit opens the Kingdom to us as He reveals Himself to us. The potential to live out the highest life is never realized until the Kingdom is discovered within. The Kingdom is not discovered within until we reach a point in our cross-bearing journey that we encounter the Comforter in such a way as to have Him open the Kingdom to us.

Sixth Station: Jesus Falls The Second Time

Carrying our cross is difficult and will result in falling. At times the weight of our circumstances and pain will be overwhelming. Furthermore, our human nature and fleshly desires will rise up and cause us to stumble. Knowing your carnal nature will fail you while traveling on the road to resurrected life will help empower you through. You ALREADY HAVE been made the righteousness of God in Christ. Just because you're not acting like it, doesn't mean you're not already righteous. A seed doesn't deny its essence because it doesn't instantly manifest what it's carrying. Stop living in shame and throw off guilt and condemnation. Rejoice in the fact that God made you a seed carrying righteousness. Your nature and essence became righteous the moment you received Jesus. He performed a legal transaction whereby He took your sin and gave you His perfection. You are positionally in right standing with God, now and forever. Receive this inheritance and the next time you fall, use the crutch of Jesus' legal transaction to lift you up. Your emotions will keep you on the ground. Until they come under your legal nature, they will fight against the Spirit and all that's been given to you in the great exchange. Seek the pathway where your true self begins to germinate. Keep your mind fixed on your righteousness in Christ. This will empower you to get up after every fall.

Remember to cultivate the habit of focusing on your future. As you contemplate the visions, dreams, and prophesy over your life, you will diminish the pain of falling and even wipe it away. No matter how many times you fail and fall, getting up is all that's needed to keep you on the path to resurrection. What you focus on is magnified. Condition your mind to focus on things above not on fleshly things. Condition your mind in your righteousness and rest in the fact that "Though the righteous fall seven times, they rise again ..." (Proverbs 24:16a).

Seventh Station: Jesus Meets The Women Of Jerusalem

"Jesus turning to them said, 'Daughters of Jerusalem, do not weep for me, but weep for yourselves and for your children. For behold, the days are coming when ....'"

Luke 23:28, 29a

There will be times throughout your journey to the resurrected life where you will be greeted with temptations to pity yourself. Arguments will arise that will tempt you to weep for yourself and feel sorry for what is happening to you. Be aware and as you encounter such opposition to the cross, disengage from it and refocus your gaze upon the future. Say to yourself, *"behold the days that are coming."* Allow your intentions to shift your focus to the resurrected life. Turn inward and begin seeking the Kingdom within, anticipating a reconnecting in the realm of Kingdom consciousness. Your emotions will want to entertain the pity party, using it as a means to escape from the cross-bearing experience. Stand up and place your emotions under your Will by taking your thoughts into the future. Become inwardly violent and take back your emotions. Engage the eyes of your understanding on God's promises to you. Don't allow your emotions to govern your soul and body. Remember, you are a legal human with emotions, not an emotional human. The more you live out of your legal nature which is part of your divine nature, the more effective you become at carrying your cross. It's not possible to carry a cross when living out of your emotional self. Not until your emotions are placed under the governance of your legal self will they allow you to carry such a destructive tool to the flesh.

Perseverance elevates you to a position whereby overcoming the self-life is possible. This is a necessary character trait to cross-bearing, especially in times where opposition to the cross rears its ugly head. There may be no greater and more effective way to cast down such opposition as engaging your Will and intention to persevering. Holding onto perseverance, wait in patience for the test to pass and anticipate a host from Heaven bringing comfort for your weary soul. All circumstances which place the cross on your back becomes a ladder of ascension. To all who are in Christ, this ladder of ascension takes you into places only discovered by those carrying a cross. This is where we are presented with the invitation to the ascended life—a life of heavenly attributes rooted and grounded in the realm of Kingdom consciousness. It's a life of unique realization and unattainable closeness to Christ apart from the cross' work in our lives. There are riches untold made available to only those who allow the cross into everyday life. The Apostle Paul received a grace and a power Jesus extended to him that could have only been found and accepted in the midst of great suffering (2 Corinthians 12). Look for Christ to extend His special grace in your times of great suffering. Put out your hands of surrender and anticipate a love to be placed in them which ignites a power to persevere like nothing you've imagined.

Eighth Station: Jesus Falls a Third Time
Ninth Station: Jesus Clothes Are Taken Away

As you continue to rise from falling, encourage yourself in the Lord. Look for Jesus to reveal Himself to you in unique and special ways. Knowing patience needs to have its perfect work, be aware that you are closer to your death than your last fall. Trust the Lord with all your heart and lean not onto your own understanding. Rather, in all your ways, acknowledge Him as being the one directing your path. Know that your steps are ordered of the Lord and He is in full control of every circumstance and situation. Beware of shame and its attempts to derail your cross carrying. The world will "take away" your clothes and strip you naked in attempts to cause shame to replace humility. If they succeed, recognize it and clothe yourself with humility and longsuffering. Humbleness is an item of clothing that will enable nakedness to occur in any and all situations. Jesus *"made Himself of no reputation"* by clothing Himself in the garments of humility. This empowered Him to despise the shame and endure the cross. What an example for us to model!

The garments of praise are another item of clothing we need to put on. During seasons of heaviness, clothing yourself in praise removes the heaviness. The two emotions cannot exist equally simultaneously. Don't let heaviness slow you in your walk to crucifixion. There is joy in the journey to the resurrected life. There is comfort to be experienced in the midst of pain. In fact, there is a unique, specific joy only given to those on the road to their crucifixion. Some of this joy will be revealed to you as you cast down heaviness by putting on the garment of praise. Condition your mind to engage your will towards this end. In doing so, you will be lifted to a new realm of existence—the realm of Kingdom consciousness.

Stephen, in Acts 7, found this realm as it appeared to him in his field of consciousness, creating an exchange—the spirit of heaviness for the garments of praise. As you read this account, know that the realm of the Kingdom is as accessible to you as it was to Stephen. Those who faithfully carry their cross and renew their minds with Kingdom information are sure to experience the opening of this realm. There are benefits to suffering that far outweigh the pain. Perhaps the greatest is the appearing of Heaven, its hosts, and attributes within your personal experience.

> *"When the members of the Sanhedrin heard this, they were furious and gnashed their teeth at him. But Stephen, full of the Holy Spirit, looked up to heaven and saw the glory of God, and Jesus standing at the right hand of God. 'Look,' he said, 'I see heaven open and the Son of Man standing at the right hand of God.' At this they covered their ears and, yelling at the top of their voices, they all rushed at him, dragged him out of the city and began to stone him. Meanwhile, the witnesses laid their coats at the feet of a young man named Saul. While they were stoning him, Stephen prayed, 'Lord Jesus, receive my*

spirit.' Then he fell on his knees and cried out, 'Lord, do not hold this sin against them.' When he had said this, he fell asleep."

Acts 7:54-60 NIV

Tenth Station: Jesus is Nailed to The Cross

As painful as it is to be hoisted up on a cross after being nailed to it, disciplining ourselves to look past the pain is important. As you become aware of pain, connect tightly to it. Root yourself in the understanding as to why the pain is necessary, reminding yourself as often as needed of the importance of the cross. Then, with the engagement of your Will, push through the pain and wait patiently. Realization of a space within pain will begin emerging. This space is where we meet Christ. Not only Christ, but attributes of His character and presence only found in pain coming from cross-bearing. What we focus on magnifies. It is good to recognize and become aware of the pain as it helps you become disciplined in pressing through the pain. The opportunity here is to focus on something to overshadow the pain. It should be something of such treasure that it will beckon pain's appearance and awaken a cry from within, "Therefore I will boost all the more in my pain."

The more we center our attention on the pain, the more likely we will remove the nails from our hands and climb off the cross. If you have yet to discover Christ's appearing through your pain, don't fret. Continue the discipline of pressing through the pain and waiting in the space with anticipation of His appearing. Until then, know you have alternatives to strengthen yourself. The more effective you become at setting your attention and affections on visions of the future, the easier it will be to remain nailed to the cross. Jesus became so focused on the joy that was before Him that He was able to endure the cross. Receiving joy as we look into our future becomes another key to enduring our cross.

Sitting in your pain is another option worth discovering. Resting in Christ's timing is a worthwhile discipline, especially during times of trial. As you do, talk with the Lord. Engage in deep, meaningful conversation, not being afraid to grieve the present loss of your old nature being crucified. Authenticity during times of pain attracts the Lord's attention on a whole new level.

Just prior to Jesus' death, He uttered an important statement we all need to confront before our self-life is put to death. *"Forgive them, Father, for they know not what they do."* Let's search deep into the recesses of our heart, inviting the Lord to search for any unforgiveness. As it surfaces, turn to the Father and pronounce forgiveness of their transgression toward you. Don't mind your emotions; they play tricks on you. Ignore any intrusive thoughts. Forgiveness is an act of the Will, not a feeling. If you make the decision to forgive, forgiveness is extended, and you have forgiven, period.

I have seen unforgiveness, bitterness, and unresolved anger become one of the great stumbling blocks of our time. We must examine ourselves closely, trusting the Lord to bring forth any of these belief systems which produce great states of distress. At the same time, we don't want to draw things up that aren't there, but we do want to leave room for the Lord to expose and uproot these giant barriers to the resurrected life. These emotional states and conditioned mindsets are enemies to the cross. They become legal evidence in the enemies hands hindering your entrance into the resurrected life.

In your pursuit of the resurrected life, there comes a time in the dying process where the Lord reaches a commitment level with you whereby His strength ensures you remain on your cross until the crucifixion. As you become aware of His unconditional love and commitment to you, rest assured you have nowhere else to turn. Find peace in the dying process and wait with great expectation for the dawning of Heaven in your field of consciousness. Death is a new beginning. A gateway to grasp the Kingdom realm on earth. As we cultivate the discipline of dying daily, we have the privilege of entering such a gateway anew every day.

Eleventh Station: Jesus Dies on The Cross

St. John of the Cross wrote about what he called the dark night of the soul—the times in our lives where it seems all hell has broken loose and God is nowhere to be found. It feels as if you are left for dead with no hope or inspiration. Your Will for living is dry, and all fuel for life has burned up. During these times, it's important to recognize your life is not in your hands, the Devil's, or anyone else's but God's. As difficult as it may be, do your best to align yourself with the words of Job, *"Naked I came from my mother's womb and naked I will depart. The LORD gave, and the LORD has taken away; may the name of the LORD be praised."* (Job 1:21) Cry out for revelation of the Lordship of Jesus. Fall back onto the foundation of truth by recalling scripture that edifies and comforts.

Take a mental inventory to ensure you are not being governed by your emotions. Cry out for revelation of who you are and whose you are. Seek to understand the Kingdom and the system of rulership you've inherited. Assume a posture of praise as you acknowledge all things working together for good. Keep your mind off the pain and on the resurrected life that awaits you. Anticipate the Kingdom realm opening to you. Taking every thought captive, be vigilant and resolute toward your thoughts, anchoring them to whatsoever things are true, noble, right, pure, lovely, admirable and praiseworthy. (Philippians 4:8) To condition your mind to focus on such things takes your attention off the cries of your emotions and puts to death an important enemy of the cross. Cut yourself some slack. Be free to express your Will and desires to the Lord while anchoring yourself to, *"Nevertheless, not my will, but yours, be done."* (Luke 22:42 ESV)

Job persevered through his cross-bearing season in part because he took on the mindset that God was Lord of all. As the owner of everything in his life, Job was able to let go of everything. He understood that all he had and will ever have was given to him by the Lord, the Owner. Resting in this revelation became a way of life for Job. As a result, during times when things were taken from him, his emotions were in check. It was much less of an ordeal to him. The accurate way in which he perceived life empowered him during cross bearing times. We cannot underestimate the importance of "putting on the mind of Christ." Beginning to think the way He thinks not only makes the cross bearing times bearable, it enlightens us to the rewards within our cross-bearing times.

Twelfth Station: The Body of Jesus is Taken Down From The Cross

Entrance into the death of self is realized in part, by the diminishment and acceptance of pain experienced. The less pain your circumstances inflict upon you the closer you are to death. The less your emotions react to circumstances unfavorable to you, the sooner your resurrection life will manifest. Examine yourself. Take time to ask yourself if you see progress in the diminishment of your carnal responses. Identify where the Lord has been working on you and let gratefulness spring forth. Ask yourself if you can see how the cross has diminished the life of your flesh and look for evidence of such results. As you examine yourself, be encouraged as you encounter growth. The fact that circumstances aren't bothering you the way they used to is an indication the cross is having an effect on you. Rejoice! Let this awareness of progression become a catalyst for you to continue. Let it become motivation to stay the course.

As the inner life of Christ grows, you can be sure the death of your carnal self follows. Paul's confession that he died daily is an indication of the necessity for us to take on the same mindset. Unlike Jesus' meeting with death on a cross, we are called to die daily. We do not anticipate such a meeting, but rather embrace a cross that empowers and positions us to deny our fleshly nature. In Kingdom life, the Stations of the Cross are to be lived out daily. We do this with conscious and intentional effort, through the power of the Holy Spirit, to put off the old nature. Until we become conditioned to die daily, we must be intentional about carrying our cross. This is the pathway into the realization and expression of the divine nature flowing through the resurrected life.

The sacrament of communion that Paul introduced to us was not some ritual needed to be done. Rather, it was a reminder of Christ's death. Every time they partook of the body and blood of Christ, they were to remember His death. We partake of sacraments in order to become the sacrament. We receive his death in order to enter into His death. We receive his body and blood in order to become his life on earth.

Thirteenth Station: Jesus is Laid In The Tomb

You can rest assured resurrection life is knocking at the door when the existence you used to live is dead. Things that once bothered you no longer do. Activities you used to partake in are no longer part of your life. Time you wasted doing things of little to no value have been redeemed. You're now using that time building relationship with the

Lord and stepping into His highest priority for you—seeking first His Kingdom. Your priorities have shifted from fulfilling your wants to finding satisfaction in obedience to Jesus. The things that cause you to suffer are now understood as tools to further your obedience to the Lord.

You're becoming clothed in the mind of Christ as you receive information that builds the renewed mind. In a practical sense, you are stepping into the process of putting to death your carnal mind by denying its fleshly appetites. This new life sprouting from within your old self is about to take on a nature so out of this world it will confuse the minds of those who come in contact with you. The essence of who you are, the true nature opened for you at the new birth, given to you before the foundation of the world, finally has a way of expressing itself. Through the cooperation of man with God, what was once alive died and what lay dormant is coming alive. What a mystery to unfold! What a Divine sight to behold! What a most worthy practice to entertain and occupy our pursuits.

Springtime is the season when new life comes forth. This new life carries with it substance that was not present before the death and dormant cycle of winter. We all inherit new life when coming out of a cycle of death and dormancy. Becoming aware of this new life adds strength to our perseverance, enabling us to continue towards the life we are all waiting for—resurrection life.

In the cycle of life, winter is the most trying season. It is also the most rewarding. While traveling through the Smokey Mountains of Tennessee one early spring day, I was overtaken by the beauty of new life budding through the lifeless branches. I suddenly became aware of a substance coming out of this new life that I knew does not exist as the leaves mature and complete the growth cycle. A principle of life grew out of this experience—new life coming out of a season of dormancy and death will always carry with it substance that not only captures your heart but propels you to continue walking through the cycle of life. As long as we remind ourselves of this new life during dormant and death seasons, we will be empowered. Recalling the special substance God always causes to emerge out of springtime growth will drive us to more firmly hold our cross, resting in quiet assurance of the resurrected life to come.

Conclusion

There is a necessary tension in Kingdom living. On the one hand, we have entered the field of Kingdom consciousness, a virtual Garden of Eden where we walk with the Lord continually—developing sight the way He sees, perceiving how He perceives. Living in His presence in the realm of the *"come up here,"* His Kingdom is opened to our conscious experience in ways inconceivable. However, we are suffering daily at the same time. The messengers of Satan at times feels too much, and the weight of sorrows seem crushing. Our emotions are played with as intrusive thoughts attempt to bring us down. The key to abiding in the realm of Kingdom consciousness is accepting and welcoming this tension. May you find it now and become resolute in your determination to live in the tension.

Our carnal nature has a difficult time with a chapter such as this. Keeping the carnal nature alive is easier, but not nearly as rewarding and worthwhile. We find ways to justify and even blind ourselves to this fact. I want to leave you with a challenge that I pray will equip you in the cross-bearing process. It is my prayer that you become empowered all the way to the crucifixion, and begin tasting and seeing resurrection life in the Kingdom realm of consciousness. I pray that a blanket of acceptance cover you as your understanding of the cross-bearing aspect of life becomes firmly rooted in your day-to-day affairs.

In the book of Philippians, the Apostle Paul makes an extraordinary statement.

> *"That I may know him, and the power of his resurrection, and the fellowship of his sufferings ...."*
>
> Phil. 3:10a

This phrase *"fellowship of his sufferings"* is dear to my heart. In 2007, I was going through a very difficult period in my life. I had been in a season of relentless attack with the presence of God seemingly nonexistent. One evening, while stepping out of the shower, I became overwhelmed with burden. My knees buckled as I felt like someone had punched me in the stomach; I keeled over in pain. I thought I was having a nervous breakdown. At that moment, Jesus entered the room. His presence embraced me in a way I had never experienced. He said,

"Let me introduce you to fellowship I have reserved for those willing to suffer for Me." Instantly the eyes of my understanding were enlightened, and I knew what Paul meant. This revelation became a compass for me. I learned to direct my gaze onto Jesus during times of pain, looking for the fellowship reserved exclusively for those carrying their cross-suffering for the sake of Christ and His Kingdom. For all those choosing the way of the cross, may you discover the fellowship of His sufferings. It is a fellowship where the Great lover of our soul extends an attribute of Himself reserved for such special occasions.

One Final Thought

I was flying 39,000 feet above the North Atlantic. While resting in the Lord's presence, my quiet, conscious connectedness was interrupted as the Lord spoke, "I'm taking you to a secret place. A place visited by pioneers but will be settled by a future remnant. The place is called the depths of My love." I waited patiently, surprisingly not anxious. Moments later, I found myself moved to a large room. Darkness enveloped the entire space. I knew it to be empty and lifeless, lacking anything of substance. As I was searching for any form of life, I heard the Lord say, "The highest position in My Kingdom to operate from is the place of the depths of My love. The first step in entering these depths is self-emptying. This place is reserved for the purpose of experiencing the depths of My love in order that you might become an expression of this love." As soon as He finished speaking, a host of foul spirits aggressively surrounded me. They began releasing words and suggestions that I could see were landing on my emotions. This caused all sorts of fleshly responses I knew were not my own. These spirits were attempting to awaken my flesh by "throwing" at me carnal emotions and thoughts. Their goal was to inhibit me from experiencing and entering the place of the depths of God's love, thereby keeping the depths of His love from spreading on earth. Additionally, I knew this was not merely about me but was a picture of a strategy that the enemy would use to keep God's remnant from entering the place of the depths of God's love.

I could hear anger and concern coming from the unclean spirits. They were eerily outraged. I noticed death was the overwhelming substance coming out of their words. This death was directed at keeping the depths of God's love from coming to life in the heart of man. "Look at all the oppression in the world. Where is your God?" said one spirit. Another's thoughts I could hear, "Look at all the suffering on earth. What are you going to do about it? You can't sit with a suffering God; there's no such thing." A third spirit violently spoke, "This self-sacrifice, self-denying, self-emptying is not worth it." Suddenly, I realized more deeply, that the spirits were projecting these ideas into my emotions and thoughts and I was in the middle of a battle. I wrestled for what seemed to be 30 minutes. At times I became overwhelmed but could see an infusion of overcoming grace rising in me. Toward the end of this tiresome wrestling match, my awareness was directed to my emotions, and I realized calmness was dominating my inner self. Just then I was taken to a scene where I was counseling a young man. He was confessing an addiction, pouring out grief, pain, and great sadness. As he was, I felt his feelings erupting in me and a burden like never before weighed heavy in me. It was empathy and compassion awakening in me from the place of the depths of God's love, empowering me to model the law of love—carrying another's burden. I sat there and like the earth receives rain, I became one with his emotional state. I thought, "This is what carrying the depths of God's love is like."

    I took a deep breath and began taking in all that had just happened. As I did, I knew I was back in the place of the depths of God's love, but in the counseling session at the same time. Without notice, another group of evil spirits began attacking me, only this time they became more seductive and violent, agitating my senses and emotions and planting defeating thoughts. The foul spirits restarted their attempts to break down my self-emptiness. As they continued, I thought to myself, "It's too late, I have already been enlightened by a power from the age to come. Perhaps the power of all powers, the depths of His love."

    I thought my experience in the spirit was finished when I heard a voice that I knew was from the future. As the sound of his voice touched my ear, I was taken to him. When I arrived, I heard, "Remember, the place of the depths of My love is the place My remnant will learn and discover, in an accelerated manner, how to only do what you see the Father doing. Keep first things first, seek My Kingdom." Carry each other's burdens, and in this way, you will fulfill the law of love.

A Shift in Thinking

We have been conditioned to think that life has distinct seasons separate from themselves. We enjoy certain seasons while reluctantly preparing to weather through others. But what if the human experience was designed differently? What if your spiritual man was designed to live in a perpetual season of rest and peace on the mountain top of Kingdom consciousness. What if your natural man was destined to a life in the dessert season of death, never to see life this side of eternity. What if your spiritual man was ordained to be clothed in humility, effortlessly souring the heights of ceaseless joy and adventure while your natural man was destined for an eternal season nailed to a cross, where movement yields excruciating pain. Such is the life of one who discovers himself in the Kingdom field of consciousness.

What if you were destined to perish and be renewed simultaneously? I have found a place in the Kingdom realm of consciousness where, though my outer man is perishing; my inner man is being renewed. Both seasons continually in operation. The beauty of this way of life is, in the Kingdom realm, you learn to embrace the perishing of your outer man and receive the life flowing into your inner man. When Jesus said, *"Come up here, and I will show you ...."* He was inviting you into something incomprehensible to the natural mind. When Jesus said, "And I when I am lifted up from the earth, will draw all people to myself," was offering a one-way ticket to His domain—the domain where we receive the steady flow of eternal life into our spiritual man.

Prepare your heart for great change. The Kingdom is coming to you. The more you learn to live with the perishing of your natural man, the more of the Kingdom is awakened and expands to your spiritual man. The Word of God is living and active, sharp enough to divide the life of your natural man from the life of your spiritual man. You can do all things through Christ who gives you the strength.

CHAPTER 6

From Warrior to Citizen

I sat by a river, engrossed in visions of God. Leaning back, I noticed the crystal clear water. It reminded me of the organic farm experience I had in Hawaii when I saw a drop of this water on a leaf. Now, this was an entire river flowing with this unique water. I wanted to jump in, but heard a voice responding to my desire by saying, "Wait." I asked, "Why?" and the voice replied, "This is the river of the Kingdom that carries the Saints who have laid down their weapons and taken up Kingdom law books." I knew what the voice was talking about because I received this revelation several years ago and was walking in it to one degree or another. I wanted to jump in as I felt it would be a new experience. The voice spoke, "You are wise to be patient. This river is not a river to play in. Nor is it a river to jump in, out of an emotional desire. Tell the Saints they must understand Kingdom law before they can lay down their weapons." I looked down and saw a mass of people. I knew they were those who had become "Ninja Warriors," soldiers fighting for Jesus, living in a warlike mindset. I could see they developed a conditioned way of thinking that they should be "fighting" for personal freedom and the establishment of the Kingdom on earth. I also saw millions in the group wearing pilgrim attire. I thought, "These are Kingdom Saints that received the revelation found in the Kingdom law book and have laid their weapons of war down." I also knew they could not lay their weapons down without a shift in their way of thinking. I thought, "Is the change in their thinking the cause of their weapons being laid down?" Then I saw an explosion in someone's mind and knew that was a picture of transformation by the renewing of the mind. I thought to myself, "This is no small matter. We need to annihilate, literally blow up our conditioned way of thinking that we are 'soldiers for Jesus.'"

I wanted to tell the mass of people all that I had seen and learned. The Lord spoke, "This is not your responsibility. You have taken a desire of mine that I have not entrusted to you." I asked, "How Lord?" He responded, "In this realm, the works of the flesh are anything you do that you don't see Me doing." I immediately saw He hadn't given me that assignment. I agreed with Him and asked for my flesh to die in greater measure.

Another voice spoke, "You have not yet jumped into the river. When the time comes, you will know." A drop from the river fell on my tongue, and I found myself back before the throne. As I was being led back, a voice spoke, "The river is hidden from you for now. I was ordered to place a drop in your mouth. You are now a carrier of the river. Be patient and remember this moment." I thought, "How am I going to remember this?" The voice responded, "But I, whom the Father will send in My name, will teach you all things and will remind you of everything I have said to you." I remembered that to be a Bible verse out of John and became overwhelmed. I knew I was just talking to Holy Spirit. I became excited, teeming with joy. The Holy Spirit spoke, "The word of God is Alive. Take, eat, for in the days to come I will bring to your remembrance what the Father needs from you."

My attention was diverted momentarily, as I became aware of the nature of the Holy Scriptures in a way I never had. I became distracted and found myself before the throne pondering my time with the Holy Spirit and thinking that was the happiest person I've ever come in contact with. Worship erupted around the throne as I thought, "Wait a minute, how could that be. He's on the earth in the midst of sinful, hellish, lawlessness …" a voice spoke, "Are you still slow in learning? He is not on earth; He is in Heaven." Immediately, I was taken to the vision of the grass growing above the earth and the sheep flying down.

I became excited when I heard, "You are in Heaven on earth!" Then a vision flashed before my eyes of many Saints that had fallen from the realm of Heaven on earth. Soberness came over me as I realized that could be me.

I felt pain in my back, and the Lord spoke, "Fear not, for I am with you. I had gone before you and made a way in the desert." When He said that, I saw my carnal nature and sinful life before He came into me. I thought WOW! How could this be? The filth of my carnal man was so vast. Suddenly, I saw a picture of flowers blooming in the desert. It was spectacular. There were millions upon millions—blue, white, violet, purple, and yellow. My eyes focused in on an area in front of me where a valley was forged between two mountain tops. I fell backward and found myself before the throne.

As I lay there, a voice spoke. "The valley represents all those living in the 'ninja warrior' mindset. The two mountain peaks represent the two places I will take those in the valley." "What are the two mountain peaks?" I asked. I looked to my right and hovering above the mountain was the words, "Seek first the Kingdom." I looked to my left and written half way up the mountain was "seek first His righteousness." I asked the voice, "How are they going to get from the valley to the mountaintop?" There was silence and I remembered, "It's none of my business." The Lord responded, "Tell My people to seek first My Kingdom. I am about to release this revelation and you will see many leave the valley." As my time ended in this place, I heard in the distance a door opening. I returned to the throne to gather energy. I knew I would be taken somewhere once I regained strength.

Once strength came into me, I was led into a room that was pitch black. I could see nothing. The sense I felt was one of rest. I knew peace to be the essence in the blackness and I realized I was in a room called sleep. I asked the one who brought me, "Where are we?" He responded, "This is the part of the brain the Saints used to use to 'fight for Jesus' and 'fight to establish territory for the Lord.' This is its intended purpose." When he finished speaking, I saw the peace within the blackness floating to other parts of the brain, energizing it with rest and strength. The peace contained rest and sleep in the form of a vapor that was taking up space in other areas of the brain. "This is amazing!" I thought. The voice responded, "The restoration of the brain requires a change of mind. Going from the mindset of 'ninja warrior for Jesus' to 'Kingdom citizen' frees up more than you can imagine." Just then, my temples began pulsing and I thought to myself, "This transformation is looking like the brain I saw in my Isaiah 6 experience." The Lord responded, "The sons of God will inherit the mind of My Son, and once again humanity will exclaim, 'Look, there are little Jesus'!" I knew Him to be referring to the 1st century Church when they were called Christians for the first time because they exemplified, in character and action, Jesus.

I was carried away in the spirit and found myself walking East on a raised road. I felt it was the raised highway of Isaiah 35. My attention was drawn below the road, where I saw a man sitting on a bench. He was alone and looked beat up. I could tell he had PTSD. I saw he was crippled inside and out. His family had been torn apart, and he had lost all the hair on his head. He was overweight and appeared 20 years older than he was. He looked at me, and as soon as our eyes connected, he was transported to me. He stood beside me and began dancing. "I haven't walked in almost 30 years!" Joy was bursting out of him like lava shooting from a volcano. He put his arm around me and asked if he could stay. Before I could answer the man moved in front of me and the spirit of Revelation appeared in between the man and me. The man froze momentarily, as Revelation spoke "You can't tell him he's welcome here until you share the revelation and he accepts it." It was then that I knew what had happened to the man and where I was standing.

The man was a wounded war veteran from the Church of the "ninja warriors" for Jesus. All the spiritual warfare had rendered him ineffective for the coming harvest. I also knew I was standing on the revelation of "citizenship" and "ambassadorship," the identity that will replace that of a soldier for Jesus. I asked the Lord, "What am I to do?" "I brought you here because I want you to tell your family about this. Give them the revelation, and you will not only save many from this man's peril but remove many who are in his condition." When the Lord finished, I looked back at the spirit of Revelation, and he was gone. When my eyes re-connected with the man, I saw in him millions of souls crying out for freedom. I declared, "Be free in Jesus name." I saw red rain falling from Heaven and multitudes fleeing the torment of unnecessary fighting with Satan and his spirits of darkness. I knew the freedom I saw in these people were contingent upon them stepping into their new identity. "How am I going to get them on the raised highway?" I thought. A voice responded, 'Keep your mind on the task at hand. Leave my job to me." I agreed and moved on.

I asked the man if he wanted to stay here and he responded with a resounding "Yes! Will I remain healed?" "If you read this book and accept your new identity," I replied. Because his intent was towards reading the book, I saw a bolt of energy leave the book and enter his mind. He became startled, went into a trance and began quoting statements expressing his new identity. "I am a child of the King. I am a citizen of a country whose government is well able to care for me. I am an ambassador. I represent my country; I don't fight for it. I am a legal citizen, not a military citizen. The only fight is in my mind." On and on he went. Repeating the same thing the book said about him. Suddenly I was in his brain watching new connections being formed. I saw one that I knew looked like the mind of Christ being formed and heard a voice, "Write the information down and make it plain. Rapid transformation such as the world has not seen is soon coming." Everything abruptly stopped, and I was carried away to the throne where I knew I was waiting for my next assignment.

In the Kingdom realm on earth, we do not fight as soldiers. Our country, the Kingdom of Heaven, has its own army well able to defend us and the territory in which we live, and move and have our being. Additionally, all our attention needs to be on repentance-changing our minds with the information of the Kingdom. It is this act alone that sets in motion all subsequent actions necessary for the Kingdom realm to reveal itself on earth. It is only the act of the Kingdom coming on earth that causes the collapse of darkness. That's not to say we won't engage in proclaiming, declaring, rebuking and casting out. We will, only it will come from a place of victory rather than an attempt to "take ground" or "establish victory." Heaven is as established on earth as it ever will be, just not yet in human consciousness. The only thing Heaven is waiting for is humanity to become aware of its existence in ever-increasing measure. When the awareness reaches a tipping point, the present laws of darkness collapse, bringing collective consciousness to the nature of a set of laws always in existence but hidden in plain sight. The pathway to such experience is transformation brought about through the renewing of the mind with information of the Kingdom.

Thoughts Regarding Transformation from a "Soldier" Mindset to "Citizen" Mindset

I was ordained a teaching elder at my local Church in 2004 and began teaching immediately. Soon thereafter I encountered resistance from darkness and started praying. I would spend hours interceding against the powers and principalities I believed were attacking the community and our Church. I prided myself on the fact I had become a "spiritual Ninja" for Jesus. I would, in faith command these unseen powers away. After two years of persistent prayer and intercession, I realized I was getting nowhere. I saw no growth from the Church community nor were my prayers being answered. I was mad. I thought to myself, "I've spent two years working hard, praying against these demonic powers and have gotten nowhere." "Lord," I prayed.,"I've been a good fighter for you, binding and loosing, commanding and casting out, but nothing's happening." I pleaded with Him, "I've spent countless hours sacrificing time and energy on behalf of Your Church." It was even prophesied to me that I was a general in the spirit and would do great damage to the kingdom of darkness. I was perplexed, angry, and beaten up badly from innumerable spiritual attacks. I was about to give up when the Lord began speaking to me about His Kingdom ways. I began learning about an identity that is discovered in the field of Kingdom consciousness. An identity that is hidden in the renewed mind and actualized as the eyes of your understanding become enlightened. Little did I know, at the time I was functioning out of a mindset born from the carnal nature. Disguised as truth, this stronghold of the carnal mind creates busybodies; people doing something but really doing nothing. I was living out of a man-made mindset, not the renewed mindset that Jesus uses to reveal our true identity. I was engaged in activity that was birthing resentment, anger, bitterness, PTSD, and other characteristics that, if I continued down this path, would disqualify me from entering the overcomer's life.

Over the next several years I was introduced to a facet of my true identity in Christ. The Church at large is presently in transition and resides in one of two places. I discovered one Church to be in a battle because they chose to "fight for the Lord," while the other is currently rising up in the Kingdom realm of consciousness and leaving the fight to Heaven's army. The one Church is keeping alive the carnal nature and all that comes with it, while the other is learning to yield to Jesus as He builds His Church-an organism growing in the Kingdom realm on earth, preparing to harvest the crop of the ages. The Church in the Kingdom is centered on being transformed by seeking first the Kingdom. Their time and energy are consumed with Jesus' highest priority to seek first the Kingdom, knowing all that is needed for the end time Church is provided through this all-encompassing activity. These Church members are resting in the finished work of Christ, seeking to only do what they see the Father doing. Unless they are fighting the good fight of faith, attention is rarely given to the works of darkness. To live in the Kingdom realm of consciousness is to be consumed with the Kingdom of Heaven on earth, not fighting against opposition.

The following is a brief synopsis of my discoveries. My discoveries are not a theoretical proposition but rather a day to day testimony of a life lived in our identity as an ambassador and citizen of Heaven. My testimony spans many years of freedom from fighting spiritual powers of darkness while resting in my Fathers ability to care for me. It is my prayer that you, by faith, step into these higher truths while simultaneously laying down the part of your identity that propels you to feel the need to fight for yourself, the Lord and anything else.

Before I introduce my invitation to lay down a "battle" or "fighting" mindset and step into your identity as a citizen and royal family member, let me share the only New Testament scriptural grounds that I've found for fighting. "But flee from these things, you man of God, and pursue righteousness, godliness, faith, love, perseverance, and gentleness. Fight the good fight of faith; take hold of the eternal life to which you were called" (1 Timothy 6:11, 12a). Fighting to establish the right belief system is the only fight we are to engage in. The battleground is the mind. Fighting to grow and develop the renewed mind is where our efforts to fight must be focused. We cannot begin to "take hold of eternal life" experientially until we isolate our fight to the "good fight of faith"—fighting to grow the renewed mind which is the belief system of the Kingdom. Don't mistake Paul's analogy of a soldier to mean we are soldiers. He was no more calling us a soldier than he was calling us a track-racer when he likened us to runners.

Until we reach unity with Christ, our fight is in the mind. As we rise up to take back our soulish faculties and place them under the rulership of Christ in us (mind, will, and emotions), a war ensues. All deeply held beliefs within us have erected fortresses, defending themselves against the "knowledge of God," the information of the Kingdom. Some have created a stronghold while most make up our identity. When you begin meditating on subject matter outside those deeply held beliefs, you encounter friction and resistance. The fight is pressing through the emotional entanglement you will encounter through incongruence between the new thought and old emotion that created a bonding relationship with the old thought. Don't mistake the enemies attack against you as an invitation to fight. Rather, quiet yourself before the Lord and wait to hear what He says about the opposition. In my experience, the vast majority of the enemy's attacks are either a test or a tool to keep me from being proud.

Persevere. Don't give up. If you are seeking first the Kingdom, which is your chief responsibility as Kingdom citizens, you are on a plane of existence where there is no time, and God is on your side. In the Kingdom, what would take a thousand years could be done in one day. Like a song you have on repeat, play "Kingdom thoughts" over and over in your mind. Agree with God that your old thoughts are carnal and of the old nature. Confess your struggles and frustrations to your loving Father. Change the way you think because a new way of thinking has arrived-thinking grown out of the soil of seeking first the Kingdom. This way of thinking will move you positionally from a soldier on the battlefield of earth to a royal family member in a territory called the Kingdom of Heaven, awaiting colonization instructions from King Jesus.

During this transition, you will encounter forces of the kingdom of darkness. The parable of the sower speaks clearly to this occurrence. Receiving information about the Kingdom is the foundation of Satan's only threat to his kingdom losing influence. When you come under attack, I encourage the following response: First, examine yourself to see if the Lord may be "sifting you like wheat." God uses all things to work together for your good, even Satan. Ask the Lord if there is sin causing the attack. If so, repent, and move on. Secondly, know that Satan and his demons are tormentors. His nature is to steal, kill, and destroy. When he attacks you examine yourself to make sure you are in a state of rest and peace. A Kingdom citizen, no matter the circumstance, ought not to lose their state of rest and peace over anything. Once you have examined yourself, rise up in the authority of Christ in you, and tell him to leave. If he doesn't leave, get firmer and command him to flee. If he still remains, then use your right as a citizen to petition your Government. Come before the Lord in reverent prayer, let him know the details of your cause, and petition Him to render a verdict on your behalf. Rest assured you have been heard and trust the Lord's timing in response to your petition.

> *"Let us then approach God's throne of grace with confidence, so that we may receive mercy and find grace to help us in our time of need."*
> Hebrews 4:16

You are not a religious person, nor are you an emotional person; you are, first and foremost, a legal person—with rights and privileges. One of these privileges is having the country of your citizenship, the Kingdom of

Heaven on earth, protect you. The army of Heaven has a duty to protect not only its territory but all of its citizens. Rest in the Lords wisdom and strength and trust that He who has begun a good work in you will be faithful to complete it.

In my life as a citizen living in the Kingdom realm of consciousness, rarely do I rebuke the Devil when he attacks me personally. Rather, I acknowledge his presence in my life as a tool in the Father's hand. He is a tool to sift me and refocus my attention on my communion with the Lord. The Kingdom within me is my refuge. Any and all attacks from the "enemy" is an opportunity to acknowledge my state of weakness in quiet confidence that "when I am weak, then I am strong."

If you insist on maintaining a paradigm of a soldier, consider that when two countries go to war, there are two general "locations" of battle—the battleground and the courtroom. If you feel you must keep the mindset of a fighter, take your weapons to the courtroom. Consider Ephesians 6 with the eyes of a lawyer's understanding, not a soldier. A lawyer will tell you the "armor of God" has as much relevance in the courts of law as it does on the battlefield, if not more. Take a minute and read this passage closely. Read it as if you were a lawyer and ask yourself what relevance it has for a lawyer. In our culture of war and death, we identify so much with soldiers that we input ways of thinking that God never intended. However, the fact that you are a "citizen" (politician/lawmaker) of Heaven implies you are literally a lawmaker. This places you directly before the Judge in Heaven's court of law.

> *"Finally, be strong in the Lord and in his mighty power. Put on the full armor of God, so that you can take your stand against the devil's schemes. For our struggle is not against flesh and blood, but against the rulers, against the authorities, against the powers of this dark world and against the spiritual forces of evil in the heavenly realms. Therefore put on the full armor of God, so that when the day of evil comes, you may be able to stand your ground, and after you have done everything, to stand. Stand firm then, with the belt of truth buckled around your waist, with the breastplate of righteousness in place, and with your feet fitted with the readiness that comes from the gospel of peace. In addition to all this, take up the shield of faith, with which you can extinguish all the flaming arrows of the evil one. Take the helmet of salvation and the sword of the Spirit, which is the word of God. And pray in the Spirit on*

> *all occasions with all kinds of prayers and requests. With this in mind, be alert and always keep on praying for all the Lord's people. Pray also for me, that whenever I speak, words may be given me so that I will fearlessly make known the mystery of the gospel, for which I am an ambassador in chains. Pray that I may declare it fearlessly, as I should."*
>
> Ephesians 6:10-20

One final thought before leaving this passage. If this was a passage insisting we are soldiers in the Lord's army, then why wouldn't Paul be asking for prayer to be a good soldier? Instead, he asks for courage to speak (look at verse 19). Sounds more like he's asking for communication skills which are more in line with what an effective lawyer needs, not a soldier. Furthermore, he concludes his prayer with the phrase "I am an ambassador" not "I am a soldier." Remember, no ambassador ever becomes a soldier. Quite the contrary, an ambassador is granted diplomatic immunity which is, amongst other things, exemption from war. Selah.

One day I came to the realization there was no command or even exhortation to "fight" in the New Testament. The only time the Holy Spirit breathed into New Testament scripture to fight was referring to our beliefs. The only battle we are exhorted to fight is within: "this fight is a battle between our flesh and the Spirit for 'our flesh wages war against the Spirit.'" To engage in a fight outside of your inner self is not correct Kingdomology under the New Covenant. Despite this mindset being part of certain movements in theology, we have entered the Kingdom age. We are no longer subject to our theological understanding. As we enter the Kingdom realm of consciousness, we grow in Kingdomological understanding which infuses greater influence potential on earth. For those who can see the Kingdom of Heaven, who have entered the Promised Land of Kingdom consciousness, they know it's made up of righteousness, joy, and peace-not war, fight and battle.

A close look at the most referred to Scripture identifying a believer as a "soldier" shows us something. 2 Timothy 2:2-4 says:

> *"The things which you have heard from me in the presence of many witnesses, entrust these to faithful men who will be able to teach others also. Suffer hardship with me, as a good soldier of Christ Jesus. No soldier in active service entangles himself in the affairs of everyday life, so that he may please the one who enlisted him as a soldier."*

Here we see Paul drawing a parallel between a student/ teacher relationship and soldier/enlister. In the same way, no soldier entangles himself in affairs that will not please the one enlisting him, so too will a student not engage in studies outside the one in whom his teacher is teaching. We must begin identifying with our identity as a student, citizen, and ambassador, casting down the vain imaginations that have conditioned our minds with carnal ideas.

Author's Note: Several years ago the Lord asked me to read the book of Joshua. For the next month, I read it every day. However, I had a preconceived idea about the book. Before I began this journey the Lord spoke, "I want you to read the book of Joshua with the understanding that the 31 kings needing to be conquered are strongholds of the mind. Patterns of the mind that are keeping My people from experiencing the life I have ordained for them through the renewed mind." This set me on a journey that opened the battlefield of the mind in a whole new light and led me on a broader path of victory over the carnal mind.

The "Lord of hosts" is a term used widely and often in scriptures. This term describes the army of Heaven—the army of the Nation in which you have citizenship. We must ask a simple question; does the Lord of hosts need our help in military affairs or do we think the host of angels is capable? All power and authority, according to scripture, is in the hands of Jesus. Therefore, not only do I think He doesn't need our military enlistment or assistance, I wonder if He "needs" Heaven's army at all. Scripture clearly reveals that the Lord does but, in order to drive home the fact that we are not soldiers for Jesus, I wanted to bring this fact to light. The Kingdom life is a life of rest discovered in your identity as a citizen. A citizen whose Government is well able to protect, provide and care for you. In fact, if we are called into Kingdom living on earth, and the Kingdom is righteousness, joy, and peace, then certainly those are not qualities of war, especially joy and peace. Furthermore, Jesus would have never told us to "be of good cheer, for I have overcome" or "it is finished," if He intended for us to "win" battles.

The army of the Lord of hosts is not for the Kingdom. The King Himself has more power and authority in His finger than the world has collectively. In fact, all authority belongs to Him. Therefore this assembled army is not for Him or His Kingdom but for the citizens expanding Heaven to earth. Colonization creates conflict, especially when the territory being colonized was once in hand but has been taken away. Because God knew the inevitable conflict once the Saints would rise up and redeem their rightful place as rulers over earth, He established help. It is a sure-handed solution to the resistance from darkness.

The key to the Kingdom's spread is cultivating a Kingdom environment, first in the inner world of the temple—your body. Once that's being established, the influence of God moves outward according to His measure and timing. Throughout this evolution of Kingdom establishment, opposition will come. This is when the armies of the Lord of host come in on our behalf, sometimes sparked by your petition to the headquarters, Heaven. God is an ever-present help in time of need. He doesn't usually respond in our timing, but rest assured, He will respond.

> *"Are not all angels ministering spirits sent to serve those who will inherit salvation?"*
>
> Hebrews 1:14

The Kingdom of Heaven is established forever. The Kingdom of God is what's being re-established. The Kingdom of Heaven is the rule of Christ in the home country, Heaven. The Kingdom of God is the rule of Christ in the territory being redeemed on behalf of the Kingdom of Heaven. Let's look at this another way; the Kingdom of Heaven needs no army. It is fixed forever, high above darkness. The Kingdom of God needs an army because it is reestablishing the Kingdom of Heaven on a territory preoccupied with a government that will not go without a fight- the kingdom of darkness. The Lord of hosts was established by God for the purposes of helping the Saints bring awareness of the Kingdom of Heaven through the establishment of the Kingdom of God. When the Kingdom of God is established, the Kingdom of Heaven appears and expresses its governance over a specified territory.

As royal family, we are called to redeem territory and co-labor with Christ to occupy and govern the territory redeemed. At our signal are the armies of God, but we need to petition our government and trust our Kings decision-making powers. For example, if I'm under personal attack, I don't "go to war" and cast out and command the enemy to flee. That's not my responsibility. In fact, I may be losing an opportunity to be sifted, pruned, and become more like Christ. Satan's nature is that of a tormentor. However, in the Kingdom, he is chained and "off limits" to the Saints. If he attacks, rest assured it is for your good. Become mindful that pruning is taking place. Know that it's temporary and for the purpose of cutting away every branch that is not bearing fruit. Recondition your mind away from the response of rebuking him by seeing the attack as for your good. There are times for rebuking, but they are the exception, not the rule. Ultimately, the Lord will use the pruning for building up and expanding your sphere of influence on His behalf. Although we have been given authority to signal the armies of Heaven, we never consider such an act without first receiving the orders from the Lord. If you're unsure what to do, rest in the sifting of the Lord and anticipate coming out from the straining more pure and refined.

Under the present way of thinking, much of the Church believes it's called to fight. It believes it needs to battle for all manner of causes in order to be in the middle of God's Will. When you became a Christian, you entered into a constant state of warfare, whether you wanted to or not. This is the way of life for millions of believers. Sadly, unless repentance takes place, the post traumatic stress caused by fighting will disqualify multitudes from entering the promised land of Kingdom consciousness. It is well advised to rid yourself of such thinking and put your trust in the military might of your Government.

> *"Since you laid aside the old self with its evil practices, and have put on the new self who is being renewed to a true knowledge according to the image of the One who created him."*
> Colossians 3:9b-10

It's very difficult, if not impossible to be at war and step into Paul's exhortation which says, "whatsoever things are, noble and praiseworthy, think on such things." A soldier thinks about war and is conditioned to put their minds on fighting. A Kingdom citizen thinks about the Kingdom because his mind is fixed on things above. This "fixing" conforms the mind to the patterns of the Kingdom, releasing the realm of the Kingdoms appearance subjectively. The longer the realm of the Kingdom remains in your field of consciousness, the more you become conditioned in your Kingdom identity.

My wife is a therapist who has treated war veterans. It is difficult to reintegrate soldiers back into society, let alone nurse them back to a state of health. Our Loving Heavenly Father, the All-powerful God of the universe, would not ask us to fight in a war that lasts our whole life yet be emotionally and mentally healthy. That's almost impossible. Having spent 23 years surrounded by Christians who believe they are "warriors for Christ," I can attest they are some of the most unhealthy and tormented people I know. They are incapable, due to the countless unhealed wounds, of bearing the image of their Creator. The rivers of living water flowing from their bellies are contaminated with all manner of evil picked up during a lifetime on the battlefield.

I challenge you to begin adopting a new way of thinking. A way of thinking that fosters a mindset that you are Royal family, called to change your mind by seeking the Kingdom, not fighting. A Kingdom citizen must begin to build a paradigm, engraved in your psyche, which supports the notion you have the most powerful army in the universe as your protection. Remember you are a citizen called to be a conduit through which Heaven's laws are enacted on earth. You are called to duplicate the mind and character of Christ, and in so doing, bring about change that is so dramatic that the Kingdom of Heaven appears on earth as its culture and influence becomes visible.

One final argument against "fighting for Jesus and the Kingdom." The Kingdom of Heaven has been established on earth. It's an eternal Kingdom, unshakable, immovable. It was set upon the earth in Genesis 1:3 and has not been removed-only veiled from our consciousness. The kingdom of darkness has not moved the Kingdom of Heaven off earth; it has blinded humanity to it, while simultaneously awakening humanity to another system of rulership. A man blind from birth, traveling through his subdivision, cannot see the homes. To him, they don't exist. He has no capacity to visualize homes nor has he ever seen them. As soon as he receives sight, what's always existed becomes realized. What's always existed enters his conscious experience. He adds to his collective field of consciousness something that's always existed outside of his conscious experience. Jesus' commission is not to assemble an army for war. It's to assemble a classroom which provides information that brings conscious experience to something that has always existed. Our blindness to something does not diminish its existence except in our own field of conscious experience.

> *"They will beat their swords into plowshares and their spears into pruning hooks. Nation will not take up sword against nation, nor will they train for war anymore."*
>
> Isaiah 2:4

CHAPTER 7

Love

The love of God is experienced from two different realms. The carnal realm connects with the love of God but is incapable of receiving it in the manner in which the Lord intends. The essence of His love is distorted and thereby received impurely. Because of the fallen nature of man, when God's love is experienced, we receive it improperly. As the rain falls on the just and the unjust, so to does the love of God fall on our carnal and spiritual man. This awakens both natures, affording the carnal nature energy that is designed to be dead. This awakens passions and lusts of the flesh that in turn pursues the love of God for selfish motives. Jesus gathered followers and made many into disciples. The act of becoming a disciple took the disciples into the Kingdom realm where they were able to receive His love differently. The followers of Jesus were limited to receiving Jesus' love from the carnal realm which produced a craving for the satisfaction of the flesh. Both groups received the love of God—one to their own benefit and the other to the Kingdom's advancement.

Likewise, expressing the love of God happens from one of two places; the realm of the carnal world or the realm of the Kingdom. Both expressions of God's love are authentic. However one is purer than the other. The love expressed from the Kingdom realm carries substance that is lacking in the love expressed from the carnal realm. Due to the contamination of God's love flowing from the carnal realm, the love is not received in the manner in which God designed. As the Church rises into the "come up here" realm and begins receiving God's love, we discover the incomplete nature of God's love that we have been receiving in the carnal realm. It is not incomplete because the Lord has withheld but because we have been limited in our ability to receive and release His love.

I was taken into a realm in the Kingdom called joy where I found myself in a room. I knew the Holy Spirit was the only activator and mover in this room, yet I saw a family. They were working at their Father's business. The business was growing. I saw many members, all full of joy. Although I knew the Holy Spirit was accomplishing everything I saw, He was invisible and working through the family. It was the family members doing everything, but I could see that all the credit was due to the Holy Spirit. Suddenly, I realized why the family was so happy. They had understood it was Christ in them that was accomplishing the success and growth of the Fathers business. I saw them standing in worship before the throne at the same time they were being used to build the business. They were living in a state of being known as superposition—being in multiple places simultaneously. They had experienced the Love of God through obedience to Jesus' command to seek first the Kingdom.

I could see the family name was "father/son." My attention turned above, and I saw snowflakes falling. When I looked closer, I could see written on each flake the words father/son. I thought to myself, "These are members of the family I was watching." When I thought this, I heard a firm voice speak, "These are those who have been in a time of preparation." Immediately, I knew the preparation to be seeking first the Kingdom. They were falling back to earth as Heaven's nourishment for Kingdom growth. After acknowledging the beauty of these snowflakes, I heard the Lord say, "Some I have called to be apostles, some prophets, teachers, evangelists, and pastors. Let Me build My Church." Just then I realized Kingdom apostles were returning to earth. I also knew, to this point, Kingdom apostles were yet to arrive at the maturity level I'd seen in previous visions and visits to Heaven. I asked the Lord when His Kingdom Apostles, Prophets, Teachers, Evangelists, and Pastors would be on earth and found myself back at His throne worshiping. The worship was in one voice resounding, "and the Spirit and the bride say come, you are the King we want." Suddenly there was silence, and I heard a softly spoken voice say, "It takes the renewed mind and a heart overflowing with My love for the gifts in the Kingdom Church to be presented on earth. Go in love and make disciples of My mind."

God's love in us is an overflow of the renewed mind and our experiences of His love evidenced through the renewed mind. We can become expressions of God's love without the renewed mind, but the expressions lack the measure of love poured out when we enter the life realized through the renewed mind. Furthermore, the love we express apart from the renewed mind lacks the substance needed to bring lasting fruit upon the earth. God's highest and purest expression of love is added to us as we pursue the Kingdom, not love. I always wondered why Jesus would make the first commandment to love but His highest priority to seek His Kingdom. For years it appeared to be contradictory. Today I understand and have found a principle; the more I seek first the Kingdom, the fuller and more consistent the measure of my love becomes. Love can be measured and quantified as evidenced by Jesus' expression, *"Greater love"* (John 15:13). The following is an explanation of how the Lord answered my question, "Why did you make the first commandment to love but our highest priority to seek the Kingdom? If the first commandment is to love then why don't we seek love?

The short answer to this difficult question is, "You cannot love God the way He created you to love until you seek Him with your whole mind. The whole mind is the renewed mind. The renewed mind grows and develops only through the discipline of seeking first the Kingdom. Jeremiah 29:13 states, *"You will seek Me and find Me when you search for Me with all your heart."* That word "all" in the Hebrew is *Kol* and is translated "the whole." The Lord, through Jeremiah, was telling us that, when we seek Him with our whole mind, then we will find Him in the manner in which He desires to reveal Himself. Because the renewed mind is the whole mind, until we grow the renewed mind, we must conclude that whatever our preconceived notions are of God, they are fragmented and thus inaccurate. Whatever we have "found out" about God is incomplete and flawed. All experiences with God have fallen short of what He has designed for us to "find out" about Him. This is not to say that the presence of God we have enjoyed all these years was not Him. Of course not! He has been faithful to manifest His presence. However, our carnal mind, like sunglasses, has blocked a fuller expression of His light from entering our consciousness.

The carnal mind is a fragmented mind and is limited in what it finds as it seeks God. Not because God limits Himself but rather the carnal mind is limited in what it receives of the King and His Kingdom. One distinction between what's discovered with the fragmented mind versus the whole mind is the difference between finding God in the carnal realm versus finding God in the Kingdom realm. The entire earth is filled with the influence of God but only in the Kingdom realm are you afforded the joy of experiencing Him in the manner in which He desires to be known. On the mount of transfiguration, Peter, James, and John were given a glimpse of what it looks like to perceive Jesus from each realm. This testimony was chronicled, in part for us to see what the difference between seeing Christ before we fall asleep to this world versus after we awake to His world (see Luke 9:28-36).

Another example of these two worlds is when Jesus was on the boat with His disciples. While the disciples were awake to the storms, Jesus was in another world, resting and asleep to the disciples' world. The disciples awakened Jesus and He immediately took them into His world and the wind and waves ceased. (Matthew 8:23-27)

God has chosen to esteem His word above His character (Psalm 138:2). Since He has given the earth to humans and gave us the legal right to rule, He has put limitations on Himself to effect the earth directly. Because we have yet to awaken to the field of consciousness of the renewed mind, the Kingdom realm on earth, we have yet to "find" Him. The "whole" mind brings the appearance of the field of consciousness that God has placed Himself in, revealing expressions of Himself and His love in the manner in which He intended.

We can only find God, in the manner in which He desires to reveal Himself, with our whole mind because the carnal mind has blinded us from seeing Him in His true light. The god of this world has blinded the minds of unbelievers—those in whom the renewed mind is yet to be formed. By forming the carnal mind through the information derived from the tree of the knowledge of good and evil, Satan has effectively kept us from finding the Lord in His Kingdom. However, the key of knowledge-information of the Kingdom—successfully collapses the carnal mind and heals us of our blindness. The more we seek the information of the Kingdom the fuller and more mature our renewed mind grows. The fuller and more mature our renewed mind is, the fuller the Lord's nature appears to us and through us.

Let's look at the mount of transfiguration a little closer. When Jesus took Peter, James, and John up the mountain, the gospel of Luke states that when they got to the top, the disciples fell asleep. When they awoke, Jesus was transfigured. Question? Did Jesus change or did the disciples? Was Jesus transfigured or did the disciples enter a different field of consciousness whereby they saw Jesus in a different light? Did Jesus do the changing or did the disciples. The transfigured Jesus was veiled from them until they awoke to it. God is the same yesterday, today and forever. The fact that the disciples fell asleep speaks of their present condition of being unconscious to the true nature of Jesus. The moment they awoke, they became conscious to a facet of Jesus' nature they had heretofore not seen. This is a picture of what it looks like when we collapse consciousness in the realm of the carnal mind and awaken to consciousness in the renewed mind. Jesus does not change, our capacity to see Him differently changes. You cannot enter the Kingdom until the renewed mind is developed sufficiently to express the field of consciousness of the realm that is contained in the renewed mind—the Kingdom realm of consciousness.

When Jesus said, "Love the Lord your God with all your heart and with all your soul and with all your mind" He was quoting His Father from Deuteronomy 6:5. There are two ways in which to look at this passage. Traditionally we have concluded that the Lord is asking us to love Him with our "entire" heart, soul and mind. If this is our conclusion, then we strive to love Him with everything we have. We work to put our entire self into loving Him. This is not bad in and of itself. However, I do not believe this is what the Lord is asking here.

The second way to perceive this passage is that we are to love Him with our "whole" heart, soul, and mind. If we conclude that the Lord is asking us to love Him with our "whole" heart, soul, and mind, then we make a decision to grow and develop the "whole" mind. We make a commitment to seek first the Kingdom and trust the information will grow the renewed mind. Knowing the renewed mind is the whole mind, we have confidence that, the more we seek the Kingdom, the more we will develop the whole mind. And the more we develop the whole mind, the more we will enter into the experience of loving God the way He designed for us to love Him. Up to this point, we have all loved the Lord with our fragmented mind. I pray multitudes run with this revelation and begin growing the "whole" mind, making room to love God and others in a new and more fruitful way.

Just prior to God telling us to love Him with our whole mind, He revealed an attribute of Himself that enlightens us to this important key to love. In Deuteronomy 6:4 the Lord declares, *"Hear, O Israel: The Lord our God, the Lord is one!"* God is making a statement about His nature. He's identifying an important character trait about Himself—that He is "one." He is "whole." Because God is whole, in order for us to see Him in a more accurate way, we must love Him with our whole self. Our carnal man sees the Lord in a fragmented way but our whole man, or our transformed nature, sees Him as He is. These two passages, when combined with a principle I will explain momentarily, shed's further light, not only on the truth of God's word but the beauty of truth in science.

So, to encapsulate what's been explained, let's review. Deuteronomy 6:4 highlights the nature of God as being "whole." Deuteronomy 6:5 expresses the need for us to love God with our "whole" self, as opposed to our fragmented self. Now, allow me to briefly re-introduce a principle I've discussed earlier. The principle states, "We match patterns that already exist outside of ourselves through patterns we form in our mind. These patterns in our mind are formed as we receive information." In other words, consciousness occurs when our mind grows a pattern that exists outside of us. The two patterns unify and the result is we experience the unified pattern through what we call consciousness—a conscious experience. Therefore, in order to "find God," we must renew our minds with patterns that match the Lord's patterns. In order to love God, who is "whole," we must grow and develop the "whole" mind. Then the patterns match and we find God in His own image, as opposed to finding God with our fragmented minds, which is finding God with our image. This fragmented image alters His pure nature in our conscious experience. In order to grow and develop the "whole" mind we must seek first the Kingdom which is the "whole." The more we grow the "whole" mind, the more patterns we match with the Lord and His Kingdom, who is "whole." The more patterns we match the more we find the Lord in His whole state. The renewed mind contains the Kingdom, because the patterns of the renewed mind are whole. The Kingdom appears through the renewed mind as patterns of the Kingdom reach a whole state. Because the Kingdom is the essence of the Lord, to enter the Kingdom realm of consciousness is to begin our journey of discovery. A discovery of finding the Lord in the pure nature in which He desires to reveal Himself.

Keys to the Kingdom

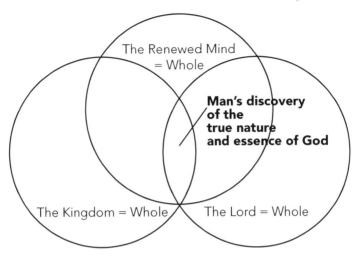

We must collapse the carnal mind. We must ascend the mountain of the Lord like Moses and stop building an image of God with our carnal minds. We must have the eyes of our understanding enlightened to the fact that we have been finding God with our carnal minds which has put gross limitations on how we see the Lord. We must begin falling asleep to the god we have fashioned and begin to awake to the God of all creation. The eyes of your understanding are the light that will lighten our path. If the eyes of your understanding become enlightened with information that grows the renewed mind, then your "whole" self will be full of light. The light of the human body is the mind's eye: If therefore your minds eye be made whole, your whole body shall emerge with an expression of "whole light" (see Matthew 6:22).

One Final Thought

Patterns of the renewed mind that match patterns of the Kingdom create an effect on earth. This effect I call a "causative by reduplication." "Causative by reduplication" is the effect of a Kingdom pattern coming into union with a pattern of the renewed mind. This effect generates a Kingdom expression on earth. Allow me to explain.

> *"Verily I say unto you, whatsoever you shall bind on earth shall be what has been bound in heaven: and whatsoever you shall loose on earth shall be what has been loosed in heaven."*
>
> Matthew 18:18 KJV

The New American Standard Bible puts it this way:

> *"Truly I say to you, whatever you bind on earth shall have [already] been bound in heaven; and whatever you loose on earth shall have [already] been loosed in heaven."*

This idea of binding and loosing through the effect of reduplicating what's already in Heaven takes place as the existing mind of Christ, in Heaven, is duplicated on earth by way of the emergence of patterns within the renewed mind. Because mind patterns are conscious experiences, a pattern from the renewed mind, when matched with the eternal mind of Christ in Heaven, creates an experience on earth— an expression of Heaven through reduplication.

Paul substantiates this principle in 1 Corinthians 2:16. The key to supporting this Kingdom law of having an effect on earth through reduplication is further understood by looking at Paul's thought, particularly a single word in this passage—"instruct."

> *"For who has known the mind of the Lord that he may instruct Him? But we have the mind of Christ."*
>
> 1 Corinthians 2:16

Here, Paul is quoting an Old Testament passage that heretofore has been used to describe the separateness of God. The notion has always been that no human has known the mind of the Lord that he may instruct him. However, under the new covenant, Paul adds a "but" to this notion and follows it with, "we have the mind of Christ." Paul brings into existence a mindset under the new covenant—the mindset of one living in the realm of Kingdom consciousness. Now, before I tie this all together, we need an understanding of this word "instruct." In the 1 Corinthians 2:16 context, "to instruct" means to set in motion a causative by reduplication. Through the effect of a pattern formed in the renewed mind, which comes into union with an existing pattern in Heaven, an effect takes place on earth. This is the Kingdom process by which the Lord "binds" and "looses" on earth.

As a side note, a causative by reduplication requires both the renewed mind as well as a *Kairos* moment of God. The need for the *Kairos* moment is our ticket to resting in His Kingdom and invites us into a deeper realization of the Lordship nature of Christ and His Kingdom. Our responsibility is to seek first the Kingdom long enough to allow the information of the Kingdom to form the renewed mind. God then has a "pool" to draw from, the renewed mind, in which He duplicates Heaven on earth in His time. In His sovereignty, He pulls out a piece of His mind from within you, uniting it with His mind and thus creating an effect—a causative by reduplication. Being involved in His plan to restore earth with Heaven is the great delight of the human soul.

In the Old Testament, when someone would ask, "who has known the mind of the Lord that he may instruct Him?" the answer would be "no one." Paul, however, received a revelation—a key of the Kingdom. He was given a principle within the law of the Spirit of life that unchains the earth, and its inhabitant's from the system that perpetuates the law of sin and death. The key is growing and developing what the disciples walked in, "the mind of Christ." Paul's answer to the question "who has known the mind of the Lord that he may instruct Him?" was "but we have the mind of Christ," not, "no one."

The following is my translation, a paraphrase of 1 Corinthians 2:16. My intent is for you to capture the idea behind Paul's thought and connect it with Jesus' Kingdom principle of binding and loosing. "Who has taken in knowledge so as to change their minds such that there is a cause to coalesce, to join together with the mind of the Lord, creating a causative by reduplication? But we, the disciples of Jesus, have that mind—the renewed mind—the mind of Christ." Put another way, "Who has known the mind of the Lord through the process of reduplicating what already exists in Heaven, by way of renewing the mind, to the point it unifies two patterns of the mind, creating a causative by reduplication?" Paul answered, "We, the First-Century Church—those who were committed to a life of devotion to the message of the gospel of the Kingdom, those who have renewed their minds with the information of the Kingdom—Disciples of Jesus!"

I pray this revelation shed's new light on Jesus' prayer to "make us one" and provides insight into the means through which to co-labor with Christ in bringing this to pass. I pray this revelation further sheds light on the fulfillment of Jesus' prayer, "Your Kingdom come on earth as it is in Heaven," accelerating movement towards stepping into our Kingdom mandate of seeing the Kingdom on earth as it is in Heaven. Selah

CHAPTER 8

Third Rung Ladder Realm

I was taken to a realm, one of the most beautiful places I'd ever been. The atmosphere was charged with something so delightful no words came to mind. I stood, took a deep breath, and in amazement was interrupted by distractions of the world beneath me. It frustrated me, and I thought, "Why the distractions?" The spirit of Wisdom appeared and said, "Because all things work together for good. Your Father knows what He's doing. Up here you learn to look at all distractions as an opportunity for you to check your status." I knew the word "status" was referring to whether or not I was "only doing what I saw the Father doing." Suddenly, the realm I was standing in opened and I received a download of information. "Now you know where you are. You will be learning to abide in this realm. You will remain as long as you do what's needed." I agreed, gave a sigh of relief, and returned to my awareness of the atmosphere.

I was hoping to see others here, so I started searching. As I began thinking of people I would like to see, the spirit of Wisdom interrupted and said, "Do not concern yourself with carnal thoughts. Cast them down. Up here, your accountability level is higher. Stay focused on learning to do only what the Father is doing." I could see others on the 1st and 2nd rung yelling, "We want to come up. Tell us how to come up." Wisdom shot a beam of light at my head that awakened a part of my brain and said, "You will teach others later—you and others. Until then, I have much to show you." I was looking forward to what she would show me when I realized something. The laser she shot at me was in the past. I knew she took me back in time and shot me. I thought, "There is no time here. I have access to roam freely." Suddenly fear gripped me, and the Lord spoke, "You do not have freedom to roam. I am Lord. You only have freedom to do what you see me doing." I agreed, bowed down, and found myself at the throne trembling in fear.

After taking a while to calm down, I thought, "How beautiful this mobile throne is." Immediately, I was led away in the spirit back to what I will call the Kingdom realm of the third rung. There I smelled an aroma I knew carried the essence of joy, the same joy in the other rungs. Wisdom responded, "You are so easily distracted." I responded, "I'm sorry, I wish I had time to explore and discover this realm." "You will have forever, once you leave Heaven in time." I agreed, and we were taken to a school. I was seated in a classroom and principles to accessing, abiding, and bringing others into this realm were downloaded into me. While the information was being downloaded, I realized each realm in Heaven is successive. Each time you leave one realm for another, the realm you leave is placed in the part of your brain written over it "identity." Wisdom spoke, "You are correct. Let the sequential nature of the Kingdom empower you to remain diligent in the seasons the Lord has you. This will accelerate the sanctifying needed for the Saints." There was a brief pause and Wisdom continued, "Come with me, I want to take you into another classroom."

Suddenly, we were in a school, an ordinary school—one I felt I would be frequenting as I remain in the Kingdom realm on earth. Wisdom and I sat down and appearing before me were men and women. I knew most of them and asked, "What are we doing." Wisdom responded, "This is the team you are assigned to." I began thinking of who I wanted to be there, when Wisdom interrupted, "It's OK to wish and desire and even express your Will. Many of the desires that surface were put in you by the Lord. For now, lay aside your thoughts and let me inform you." When she finished speaking, my attention turned to the front of the room. I saw the room expanding, and people were filling the room. Wisdom said, "Hold on. Stay in the present. I feel your excitement, but you must lean on me, trusting the Lord to keep you where He wants you. Leaving the Will of the Father gets you in trouble—big trouble." I agreed, and when I did, the room shrank back down, and the class resumed.

While surveying the room, I could see an approximate number of students. I saw the Lord Jesus looking at me. I'd never seen Him this way. He had tenacity about Him—a resolve I'd not seen in anyone before. He directed me to the wall behind the podium where the teacher stood. When I looked, I saw Jesus at the podium with Holy Spirit next to Him. Written in big bold letters was "ROOM OF THE END TIME APOSTLES." The lettering was scribed in light, blinding white light that penetrated deep down into my soul. "These letters are made of light," I thought. "Yes," the Lord responded and when He said this, I left the room. Wisdom appeared and asked, "Do you want to spend time there?" "Yes, of course." "You are welcome," Wisdom responded. When she spoke, information was downloaded in me. I felt like it was a part of Wisdom and I thanked her. "I will do my best to be a watchful, careful steward of this information," I said. Then, it occurred to me the most important character trait of the end time apostles was the daily carrying of the cross. I knew all those in the room were carriers of the cross, dying daily to everything except the Will of the Father. They all had a personal crucifixion and were living in and through resurrection life. They had no pride, fear, or carnal nature. I also knew that the sinful nature still remained in all of us but somehow, moment by moment, this group's sinful nature was in check. Wisdom responded to my thoughts as if we were in conversation, "You are correct. I will be here to help, but mostly Holy Spirit." Suddenly, Holy Spirit appeared, smiling, and full of joy. Just then, I knew I needed to know Him better and thought, "Who wouldn't want to know this Living Being!" His smile was superimposed on my face and I felt His joy. It was a joy beyond emotions—far beyond feelings and emotions. It didn't even feel like it came from my emotions. My mind began exploring where it came from, and Wisdom interrupted, "In your downtime, ponder such beauty. Until then, let's go. I have much more to show you." I felt like we were going on a journey to change the world. I got excited, positioned myself behind her, and anticipated movement. Wisdom turned around and asked why I was behind her? I responded, "It's my nature that positioned me." She responded, "You are correct, but parts of your nature are carnal still." When she said this, I realized many neurosynaptic connections in my brain were still wired to my carnal nature. I agreed with her and when I did, those connections pertaining to this instance became unwired. Simultaneously, a new set of connections formed that moved me beside her.

"That's better," Wisdom replied. I thought, "This is amazing! Changing my thoughts changes both my position and behavior. What if I could go back in time, and change everything that produced carnal connections?" Wisdom replied, "Be it unto you according to your faith." When she spoke, informational keys were downloaded in me for a special type of healing. "This information is to be sealed until it is active. Once activated tell the people in the Apostolic classroom." I thought, "I'm receiving information that could kill me!" Wisdom laughed and said, "You haven't seen the nature of Hell. All of humanity has had Hell desiring to steal, kill, and destroy. Every second, you have a death sentence on you. The only death you would experience would be caused by you. You must remain carrying your cross. You must learn to accept all hardships as a process of ensuring resurrection power remains. All Kingdom citizens must embrace this, especially as you ascend the Kingdom ladder." I looked and saw much more than the three rungs I was aware of and said to myself, "I thought we were in the end times. I thought the world as we know it was coming to an end in the next 30, 40 or 50 years." Wisdom responded, "This world, the Kingdom realm, will never end. Don't get distracted; we have much more to learn. Stay in the Fathers Will. For you, that's not the future. I agreed and was taken before a door that appeared very old.

This ancient door opened and in the room was the blood of the martyrs. I saw millions of souls who didn't die a natural death. Wisdom spoke, "This is a room where those that have endured the cross to the end find themselves one last time. I looked and saw uncountable crucibles. I saw the apostles of old all spent time here except Judas. I saw him in another room crying. I had compassion on him, but Wisdom redirected my attention back to the room. I gathered my composure, and she began showing me to what level a Kingdom Saint needed to "die" in order to function as an apostle. She downloaded information in me and touched my vision. When she did, my sight was redirected to the crucibles, and she began speaking.

"Don't concern yourself with those who call themselves apostles and are not. Don't concern yourself with those who can build good businesses under the title of apostle. You seek first the Kingdom and desire character development. Seek to discover those who will function as an apostle and pray." The spirit of Wisdom continued, "Look at the crucibles." When I did, I saw faces of individuals in the crucible. I became fearful. I didn't want to see the faces out of fear I wouldn't see those I wanted to see. Wisdom responded. "I will keep the faces from your eyes for now. Let Holy Spirit disconnect these carnal connections that are releasing such thoughts. When He does, I will show you the faces. Until then, I have put them in you."

I could see the crucibles were in the identities of the Apostles. They carried them around and were in them every day. Their heads were of normal temperature, but everything else was in the heat. I saw a man whose finger was on a switch, and I knew he was turning up the temperature at the command of the King. This man was full of grace. I wanted to visit with him when suddenly my back began hurting. "You are not minding the things of the Lord. Remember to do only what you see your Father doing. You will have eternity to discover up here. Until then, keep in mind, only what the Father is doing and go in the strength of the Holy Spirit." I agreed and was whisked away.

I asked the spirit of Wisdom if she could teach me to stay in time, but abide in Heaven which I knew to be outside of time. She responded, "That's not for me to answer. I understand your desire, and all I am free to tell you now is consider your awareness of time a blessing. Time is an opportunity to learn only to do what the Father is doing. Up here, it is an easier thing. But on earth, the Lord is getting to use you to influence earth for His sake." When she said this, I was taken to a room where I experienced "waste" leaving me. After the waste left, I heard the Lord speak, "Take the information you've received the past ten days, finish it and publish it. This is My heart for many in the coming years. The three rungs are where My Will is resting. My attention and devotion is centered on those seeking first My Kingdom, seeking first My righteousness, and seeking only to do what you see Me doing. The first two are the most important. Those on the third rung will need the seminal information I've released to you. You will need to gather with those entrusted with third rung information. The time-line is in My people's hands. I am here for you. Tread carefully in this hour. Lean on Wisdom; she will prove to be of use in limiting collateral damage." When He finished speaking, I felt an urgency to go back and write. Wisdom spoke, "You will be connected with others who have seminal Kingdom information. I will let you know who they are. Stay close to your spiritual family." I agreed and was taken to a place that brought me to tears. Wisdom responded, "Keep this sealed and know that all who walk as overcomers will not have to concern themselves with this." I felt reassured and she took me back to rung one and two.

Michael Gissibl

Transference in Unity:
Kingdom Sharing/Kingdom Commonality

    Years ago I was in a prayer meeting, and a woman began praying. She was communicating with God as if He was a loving Father to her. I never heard anything quite like it as I had yet to encounter God in such a way. As I was marveling at her intimate communication and authentic heart's expression, the Lord spoke, "My Kingdom's currency is faith, exchange your faith for your sister's revelation and the seed of her revelation will be planted in your belief system." As I felt a faith from Heaven enter me, I engaged my Will towards that end, and immediately a shift took place. Something was added to my identity, and I began experiencing God, little by little, as an unconditionally loving Father—my loving Father. Shame and guilt began diminishing, and their effects became less impactful. Immediately I stopped hiding from God when I did something wrong or wanted to do something I knew He wouldn't approve of, and instead ran to Him. I would talk to Him honestly and openly about my fleshly desires and weaknesses. To my surprise, shame, guilt, and fear largely dropped off me, and I was free to communicate with my Father. This perception of God, discovered by a mere transaction of my faith for her revelation, transformed my life. Today, I have full assurance in our Creators' unconditional love towards His creation.

    About 15 years later, I gave a chapter of one of my books to a friend. As he read it, according to his testimony, he felt the information from the book going into him. As he came out of this experience, he realized new information had been downloaded in him to such a degree that he said he could re-write a book he had been working on and was almost complete. He emailed me, telling me about this experience and I began meditating on it. What I felt the Lord share with me, I believe will change not only the ideology of the Church as it relates to "unity of faith" and "unity of mind," but its collective influence on earth. Before I share, I need to add one more Kingdom encounter.

    As I was reading my friend's email, I was transported into a realm where volumes of books sit, waiting to be written. It appears three or four might have fallen into me. I believe it to be a realm of the "Oracles of God" or a Heavenly library with hundreds if not thousands of books waiting to be written. It felt like this place was in the mind of Christ.

In this realm, I could see there is revelation untold, mysteries beyond thought, and comprehension waiting to be picked up and brought into existence. I'm not sure if I entered this realm, it was downloaded into me, or perhaps I'm just visiting. It seems, as you enter a Kingdom realm, you become what's contained in that realm as your awareness takes on added life. This realm is beautiful beyond description. It's clear to me the glory and splendor of the Lord will be revealed in and through His temple as the Kingdom realm is opened to the Saint's. Both the individual and corporate body of Christ is indescribably filled with unstoppable influence and authority. This Kingdom is BIG!! Much bigger than I'd ever imagined and He's got EVERYTHING under His control!!

Another incident took place while reading the email. My friend wrote, "it absolutely exploded my mind," and when I read that, something happened to the back of my brain, perhaps the parietal lobe. Neither the experience nor the feeling was like anything I had ever felt or could identify with. Even as I write now, I have no language to explain it. The best I can do is say I felt a billion tingles within that specific part of my brain. There have been three benefits I've discovered since the experience. My writing has gone to a new level. My Kingdom experience within the Kingdom realm of consciousness has gone to another dimension, and my soul and body have experienced a measure of cleansing as evidenced in my use of time. All this has taken place because two individuals seeking first the Kingdom came together. The convergence of two or more individuals with measured amounts of the renewed mind make way for expressions to come forth from the unity of mind.

Sometime after these experiences, the Lord began speaking to me as to the foundation of what caused Him to release this Kingdom key to accelerating unity within Jesus' Church. The foundation was, in the Lords words, "Two disciples coming together." Two Saints seeking first the Kingdom for an extended season of time, when they come together, are given the grace to exchange the divine nature within. This is not a Kingdom key to take lightly, nor is it a key to dismiss. All those who find themselves in the Kingdom realm of consciousness are living in the domain of Jesus. This realm has an operating system different from the one we've been conditioned in. Up here, all laws are subject to the rule of Christ within and are activated upon His command and timing. In the Kingdom realm, we have no Will except to only do what we see the Father doing. If your Will is still governing you, then you have no part in this gift-yet. Give the Lord permission to synchronize and unionize your Will to His and when the time is right, He will commission you with discernment. Having said this, let us be mindful and vigilant of the Lord's desire to add to our divine nature through the divine exchange. The gift is awaiting all who are in the process of being conformed to the image of Christ.

One final thought on the matter. Keep in mind that this is not about you. God has a plan and a purpose and needs to include you. However, He cannot use anyone who is carnally minded, "for to be carnally minded is death." (Romans 8:6a) Ask the Lord to make you spiritually minded, for to be so is to receive a flow of life responsible for transforming you into the image of Christ. To be spiritually minded is to have been stripped of any thought regarding our own Will and desire. To be spiritually minded is to be rooted in the renewed mind which is taken over by a field of consciousness that pursues the King, His Kingdom and only doing what you see Him do.

Author's Note: I believe we have stepped into uncharted waters, at least waters not seen since the early Church fathers. Revelation that continues to be downloaded as well as experiences in the Kingdom are providing a template for the Church to "come up here," not as an experience, but rather a way of life. We must lay ourselves on the altar and enter the discipline of dying daily. For the earth is waiting for the manifestation of the resurrected ones.

> *"Until we all reach unity in the faith and in the knowledge of the Son of God and become mature, attaining to the whole measure of the fullness of Christ."*
>
> Ephesians 4:13

After Jesus spent 40 days speaking to the disciples about the Kingdom, He was "taken up, and a cloud received him out of their sight." The disciples returned to Jerusalem and went to the upper room where they "all continued with one accord in prayer and supplication." (Acts1:14a) The phrase "one accord" means *"with one mind"* and is the same word used in Acts 2:46: *"And they continued steadfastly with one accord in the temple, and breaking bread from house to house, did eat their meat with gladness and singleness of heart."*

All the believers were one in heart and mind. No one claimed that any of their possessions were their own, but they shared everything they had (Acts 4:32). Although there is certainly an element of individuality within the Church, there is no individuality in the Kingdom. The mindset is one of union. Therefore, when the Church finds itself in the Kingdom, the individual *"temple of the living God"* becomes unified as one "member" finds another. They come together in a literal sense. There is a type of infusion, a coming together. Much like the seed of a man joins the egg of a woman forming one living being, so too does two or more Kingdom citizens come together and become unified. The major difference is in the Kingdom: unification is at the King's discretion. I believe the degree of unification that takes place is determined by how in sync the individual members are—how unified their minds have become and are becoming. Those devoting themselves to "seeking first the Kingdom" will enter into the unified Kingdom Church Jesus is building and be partakers of the divine nature experienced only in the Kingdom Church. The discipline of seeking first the Kingdom is the main ingredient and sure foundation used by the King to grow and develop union. It must be clear—it is God and God alone—who determines when and to what degree character traits are transferred and distributed. Always, always, remember: in the Kingdom realm you don't take anything, you receive. The posture is one of confident trust, patient expectation, and a readiness to receive. In the Kingdom you own nothing, yet have access to everything, trusting Him to be your provider. It is the renewed mind within us that enables us to experience such Kingdom keys of transformation. It is seeking first the Kingdom that grows the renewed mind in us.

> *"And by the hands of the apostles were many signs and wonders wrought among the people; and they were all with one accord in Solomon's porch."*
>
> Acts 5:12

The present Church's way of demonstrating signs and wonders is to seek first faith in miracles until they reach a level where their faith expresses signs and wonders. This can and often does lead to soulish behavior at minimum and usually witchcraft, sorcery, and emotionalism. In the Kingdom it is different. Through the collective gathering of like-minded "seekers of the Kingdom first," God, who longs to display

His Kingdom on earth, dispenses through the body of Christ as He chooses. To the degree we are yielded to the life of the Kingdom, seeking only to do what we see the Father doing, is the degree we will experience Kingdom realities on earth. The gift of healing is something given to you and becomes part of the Divine nature, much the same as hospitality, peace, and serving. We must lay down our pursuits of the attributes of the Kingdom and seek the Kingdom itself. Then the attributes will grow out of our development in the Kingdom.

In order to capture the minds of those outside the Kingdom, we need miracles to be present in our midst—authentic Kingdom character filled miracles. When the effect of something invisible manifests, it draws the onlooker to pursue the cause. It awakens, at the subconscious level, a holy curiosity put there by our Creator. This prepares the brain to receive, at its highest level, the message we need to present immediately following the signs and wonders—the message of the Kingdom. A beautiful illustration of this is Acts 8:6, *"And the people with one accord gave heed unto those things which Philip spoke, hearing and seeing the miracles which he did."* Additionally, Acts 1:1 states, *"The former treatise have I made, O Theophilus, of all that Jesus began both to do and teach."* It is essential to Kingdom living to teach the message of the gospel of the Kingdom, but it is necessary to express an effect of the Kingdom so that you can introduce the cause. First, you demonstrate, which opens the mind and provides an avenue for the message to penetrate most effectively. Then you preach the Kingdom This additionally opens the mind of the observer to multiply the effect. Those who demonstrate the Kingdom and teach the Kingdom will be the greatest teachers of our generation. Not because of the demonstration of power, but because of something that happens to the observer's brain, enabling them to receive more efficiently and effectively. All praise and all glory belong to our Creator. No man can boast a single thing, for behind every good work of man, stands the hand of Omniscient, infinite wisdom.

The Church needs to begin to "come up here" and present herself available to the King for unification purposes. One way to hasten this process is a conference or roundtable setting. Finding those who carry the attributes of a disciple (as laid out in my previous book) will prove to be the ones ready for Kingdom Saint unification. Present our understanding of Kingdom living at these gatherings, and I believe the Lord will begin doing things similar to my experience with my friend.

These things are similar to what we find happening in the Book of Acts. Additionally, those seeking first the Kingdom will experience more "unifying" than those carrying only the attributes of a disciple void of seeking first the Kingdom.

The Church in the Kingdom realm of consciousness is made of individuals with primary gifts, whose responsibility is to die to self to such a degree that Christ in you takes over that gift. As Jesus begins establishing His Kingdom outwardly, that primary gift is not limited to the individual. As needed, *"Christ in us"* takes on other gifts. God gave some to be Apostles, prophets, etc., for the purpose of building up the Church, but Christ operated in all gifts as the Father needed. So too will the end time body of Christ under the influence of the Kingdom of Heaven. In our generation, we will see the Lord high and lifted up on the throne of man's heart. The cleansing work of the cross will culminate in a son of God walking the earth in a manner similar to Christ our Lord.

Additionally, Jesus demonstrated this principle to Nathanael in John 1 when He said, *"You believe because I told you I saw you under the fig tree. You will see greater things than that."* He then added, *"Very truly I tell you, you will see 'heaven open, and the angels of God ascending and descending on' the Son of Man."*

> *"All the believers were one in heart and mind. No one claimed that any of their possessions was their own, but they shared everything they had."*
>
> Acts 4:32

This is a beautiful illustration of the Church sharing all possessions in order that none would lack. But look closely at the passage. *"All believers were one in heart and mind."* The Kingdom Church holds all things together, and where there is lack, that which is lacking is freely given through divine transference by faith. It is admirable to give physical possessions to those in need. It is divine to give spiritual gifts away. In other words, it's natural to give away the physical and supernatural to give away the spiritual. Both means of giving are equally present in the Kingdom Church. This requires a deep understanding that your life is not your own, but is for the collective use of Christ and His Church, for the purpose of building up the new man. As we grow and develop as Kingdom dwellers, we must come to grips with the "speeding up" nature within the Kingdom and begin accepting the divine transference of gifts. It is precisely in this place; we discover what the book of Acts Church realized as *"all believers were one in heart and mind."* Make it your nature to trust the Lord to transfer gifts and character as needed. Don't let your soul rise up or you've entered the Devils playground. Die daily, resting before the Lord, waiting on Him. If He prompts you to lay hands on someone, then, by all means, do so. The Lord is gracious and compassionate, slow to anger and rich in love, but He despises selfish ambition, strife, witchcraft and all soulish activity. It is a fearful thing to fall into the hands of the living God. Trust and obey, for there is no other way.

> *"But you, Daniel, roll up and seal the words of the scroll until the time of the end. Many will go here and there to increase knowledge."*
> Daniel 12:4

The Church is in its "greatest awakening" since the first century. The catalyst to this awakening is the keys of the Kingdom. The keys of Kingdom knowledge are primarily hidden in the field of *"seek first the Kingdom."* For the treasure is found in the field of "seeking first the Kingdom." If you are not taking steps towards seeking first the Kingdom, put this book down and cry out for a heart to do so. Ask the Lord for mercy to persevere through the enemy's enticing attempts to pull you away from this most prized of activities. There is no other pursuit left for man. We are in a transition phase into the Kingdom realm of consciousness. Seeking the Kingdom first will jump-start the transition that will transport your mind into the realm of the consciousness of the "come up here." All other roads lead to trouble since they are merely parts of the Kingdom. This is not the Lord's way. His way is the way of the Kingdom first. In the coming years, we will realize the importance of seeking first the Kingdom to such a degree that we will form schools around such an activity. The school of Kingdomology will begin replacing the schools of theology, and in turn, prove to be a major pillar in the transformation of individuals, communities, cities, and eventually nations.

A close look at the ministry of Jesus could be viewed as the launching of the first school of Kingdomology. By viewing His ministry in this light, we become empowered with understanding that shed's light on the model in which He used to awaken this Kingdom school. This school laid the foundation for the Kingdom's culture to be expressed. Simply put, Jesus gathered a dedicated group and taught them the message of the Kingdom. This placed the group in the position of actively seeking first the Kingdom. This posture eventually transported the disciples, through the renewing of the mind, into Christ's realm of domain on earth. This realm became their new space from which they lived—the Kingdom territory on earth. In a very real sense, they were born again, only this birth was not in this world—the carnal realm of consciousness. Rather, they were born into the Kingdom realm on earth. What followed was an existence that expressed the culture and influence of Heaven everywhere they went.

The Apostle Paul pioneered the second school of Kingdomology. Its intent was to rise up a company of students that would be sent out to express the culture of Heaven on earth, thereby transforming cities with the attributes of the Kingdom. We are nearing the dawning of other schools of Kingdomology that will graduate students who will pick up where Paul and his students left off. The appearing of the Kingdom age is upon us. Prepare to become part of that group commissioned to make students out of cities for Heaven's sake! Today, count the cost of entering the school of Kingdomology and start seeking the Kingdom. The sooner the Lord finds groups seeking first the Kingdom, the sooner He commissions us to be about His business.

As the body of Christ, in order to bring fuller expressions of the glory and influence of Christ on earth, we must begin working towards "unity of mind" formed from seeking first the Kingdom. It is the seed that contains God's hand for implementing unification of believers in the Kingdom. It will only come to pass as we lay down our pursuit of the "parts" of the Kingdom in exchange for seeking the whole.

> *"May the God who gives endurance and encouragement, give you the same attitude of mind toward each other that Christ Jesus had, so that with one mind and one voice you may glorify the God and Father of our Lord Jesus Christ."*
>
> Romans 15:5

There are two types of transference. The first is illustrated in the book of James: *"Is anyone among you sick? Let them call the elders of the Church to pray over them and anoint them with oil in the name of the Lord"* (James 5:14). Here we see a healthy leader in the Church exchanging sickness with health. This occurred as a result of a belief system that opened a pathway to seeing Kingdom culture expressed. This exchange takes place and is a valuable attribute of Heaven given to the Church. This measure of faith, the measure of faith which makes visible the invisible, is an important component to drawing multitudes to the message of the gospel of the Kingdom. As we approach the dawning of the Kingdom, we can anticipate such faith being expressed regularly.

The second type of transference, however, is reserved for the end time Kingdom dwellers and is exponentially more effective in co-laboring with Christ to bring awareness and expansion to His Kingdom on earth. That's not to say the laying on of hands will be done away with. No, not at all. Any time an effect of the Kingdom can be realized, the door to the Kingdom has swung wide open. The moment that happens preach the message of the gospel of the Kingdom. Be ready in season and out. Exhort all under the sound of your voice to seek first the Kingdom.

In January of 2016, I was taken in the spirit to a place where I saw a man. He was standing in what appeared to be space. I knew him to be living on earth. As soon as I became aware of him, I became aware of what I call the Kingdom principle of transference. Immediately, I saw different attributes of men of old coming into him from different directions. The men of old were literally walking into him, but I knew this represented their attributes coming into the man. At that moment I realized it was the giftings and anointings from these Saints of old coming into this man by the Lord's doing. I asked the Lord if this was true and He responded, "The mantles that man is presently running after pale in comparison to the mantles I have stored up for My crucified ones." As I pondered the enormity of this principle, I became grieved for all who are pursuing others' mantles for their own gain. "Even the ones doing it for the right reasons," I thought. "They are limiting God's best and slowing down the Kingdoms expression on earth." At that moment, I faintly realized that I was one of them and had great sorrow.

I believe we are in the beginning stages of witnessing the sons of God on earth. The Mighty Ones are coming! The Kingdom Dwellers are discovering their identity in the Kingdom realm of consciousness and in doing so, are being clothed with Kingdom attire. The overcomers are being prepared to rule and reign with Christ on planet earth. Eyesight in the Kingdom is providing entrance into awareness of the keys of the Kingdom. The keys have always been here—never hidden from us, only hidden for us. This key of transference is one principle of the Kingdom that the Lord is beginning to use to hasten what Isaiah saw on earth—the Lord cleansing and filling His temple (Isaiah 6:1-3). Only those who are lifted into the Kingdom realm on earth will have opportunity to experience Kingdom living. Eat the scroll of seeking first the Kingdom. As you do, God releases the nutrients needed, and the contents begin to digest in you. The result will be ever increasing expansion of the Kingdom within. As the Kingdom expands within, anticipate the Lord releasing you to become a conduit of Kingdom expression on the earth. It's only those who allow God to establish His throne within that will become those expanding Kingdom consciousness from the invisible realm, into the visible Kingdom realm on earth.

CHAPTER 9

Authority

Wisdom began speaking, "Anyone concerned with carrying authority, rebuke in love. There is no time to concern yourself with this. God has all authority and will dispense the authority in His time and potency. The role of leaders in the Kingdom is to give all attention, focus, and devotion to seeking first the Kingdom of God and His righteousness. They are to then instruct in like manner, teaching the Kingdom and exhorting all under the sound of their voice to seek first the Kingdom. As leaders move from venue to venue, the place where civil cases are heard, I will be with you all to reveal the measure you are to pour out. Stay focused on dispensing information flowing from seeking first the Kingdom of God and His righteousness. Anyone you identify seeking first the Kingdom is a candidate to becoming a teacher. When you find one such person give ear to my instruction. All those seeing and experiencing the Kingdom, as long as they have no besetting sins, needs to begin learning the Fathers righteousness. Tell those in this realm to avail themselves to the refiner's fire."

Wisdom continued, "Those I am preparing for an apostolic function need to father those on rung one and two. Keep in mind always the significance of the hour which is gathering all those actively pursuing 'seeking first the Kingdom.' Tell them where the lost sheep of the house of Israel gather to prepare messages of seeking first the Kingdom. As messages are prepared, the host of Heaven will be released to speed up time on behalf of the Kingdom." I became distracted, wanting to give this information to a friend. I repented and reengaged with Wisdom. "Your sin has caused me to stop for now. By the grace of God He enabled you to hear this much which is enough for the leaders of the Kingdom movement to appropriate. Publish this and I will direct you to disperse it." Suddenly, I became aware of the King's presence and began worshiping.

The Lord began speaking, "Wisdom is correct. Those pursuing authority are in danger of disqualification. Those focused on carrying the cross, seeking first the inner Kingdom, and letting Me establish My throne within, are those with the brightest future in My Kingdom." I asked the Lord, "What do you want me to do with those pursuing authority?" Stay in tune with your personal assignment and the collective season within the Kingdom." I knew what He meant and bowed in utter amazement of His love, majesty, and altogether separateness. While worshiping at His throne, the Lord spoke, "You may stay here as often as you'd like or you can take the throne with you in experience. I have much work for My leaders. I will use every second to establishing My throne within so that I may reestablish it on earth." As He was speaking, I saw Him working on the Isaiah 6:1 temple, both individually and corporately.

Wisdom then appeared and began taking me to a place, when I was interrupted by earthly things. I was shown a man who had strife written on his forehead. I saw him attempting to share the Father's love with humanity. I saw him warning the people to flee emotionalism and embrace the cross. I saw him doing all the right things only he was still on earth. He was still of the world and had yet to be transported into the realm of the 'come up here." I asked the Father if I could tell him to "come up here." He replied "No". After He spoke, I knew I would see him "up here" soon. It was then I realized Almighty God was preparing a large group of people imprisoned in the earthy Church for transportation into the Kingdom Church. I saw they were part of the Kingdom Church though they had no sight in the Kingdom realm yet. I then saw awareness of the Kingdom growing and a sweeping wind blew many into visions of the Kingdom realm. I was reminded of the prophecy, *"in the last days, God says, I will pour out my Spirit on all people. Your sons and daughters will prophesy, your young men will see visions, your old men will dream dreams."* (Acts 2:17) There were several winds that picked up those in the earthly Church and brought them into the Kingdom Church. I felt the time was not yet and became concerned. I felt the present leadership was not ready. Wisdom responded, "Keep your task in mind. Let the host of Heaven do their job." I agreed and found myself in what I knew to be the earthly Church.

Wisdom met me and began sharing, "Don't be discouraged son of God." I remembered all the benefit to be had down here and was encouraged. My desire turned and I asked Wisdom, "Could you please send me a friend who sees in the Kingdom realm of consciousness? A friend I can talk with, hug, and exchange the realities of Heaven with. A peer, not an underling or student." She responded, "You have been in a long season of alone time. It's not my assignment to determine if or when Kingdom Saints are joined together. I can tell you I see the future and you will be thankful you waited." I tried to see what she saw, but it was blocked from me. I believed her and we continued journeying.

I was distracted by many earthly tasks and felt frustrated. Wisdom replied, "No longer perceive these events as 'distractions'—every second of your life is ordered by the Lord. You will have plenty of time to abide in Heaven on earth, only not yet. Timing is important. Your tendency is to get ahead. That's why you have not been yoked with Kingdom Saints yet." I then realized that not having a friend all these years drove me into an intimate relationship with Jesus, opening the door for me to experience His Kingdom realm to this degree. I then saw a room being painted. I understood I was being transformed as I became aware of things. I fell before the throne where I heard a host singing "I am the apple of my Fathers eye." Awareness of something came to me as I was arrested in my thought, "Seal this information. You will use this sparingly. Not many will walk with this information." I became fearful and wished I hadn't seen what I saw when the Lord spoke, "You have become like a child. Remain humble and you have no thing to worry about."

I found myself lying beneath the throne. It was above me this time and a thought came to me, "When is the earthly Saints going to be lifted into the Heavenly Kingdom realm and when are those lifted into the Heavenly Kingdom realm going to begin seeing?" Wisdom appeared and answered, "Whenever the leaders begin teaching the Saints to seek first the Kingdom. When you see this, you will see the shift begin in the manner in which the Father designed and Jesus modeled." I asked if I could see who's ready to become "John the Baptist" teachers, preparing the way of the Kingdom. A longing to see who would bring about the change of mind responsible for transportation into the Kingdom realm rose up in me. Wisdom responded, "In time. For now keep your task at hand; pursue 'only doing what you see the Father doing.'"

Wisdom then slowly took me to a place where I was fed manna from Heaven. As I was being energized by the "nutrients" of the manna, I heard a voice say, "The rain is coming. Your father will know who to give this information to. He knows who will be the sons from his family who will begin teaching the Kingdom. Your father needs to know he should instruct his kids to tell as many outside the family to exhort to teach the Kingdom while at the same time personally pursuing the Kingdom above all. Whenever possible, teach only the whole. Forever leave behind the parts. Even if the kids don't know what you mean, exhort them to only teach the message of the Kingdom. The more they know of the Kingdom within, the more effective your family will be in establishing the Lord's Will.

I asked, "Are there any in dad's family that have been living in the third rung?" "That's not for you to know today. You will soon discover you are not alone." I sighed with relief and the voice departed my presence. Wisdom reappeared and I asked her if I could take a break. "My back hurts," I said. Wisdom responded, "That's because you are carrying things you were never intended to." I agreed and she said, "Soon you will be placed in a seat where your back will not hurt. Be prepared to extend invitations to "come up here." I was reminded of times past when I wanted to invite people to "come up here." It was a time when I was accessing the third Heavens daily and wanted others to visit with me. I could see I was full of pride at that time and Wisdom responded, "Times are different now. You will be given a mantle to bring people up here. Suddenly, Bob Jones appeared. He was so joyful that when I saw him, I began to laugh. His emotional state was more contagious than I could feel. He left quickly, but before leaving he said, "Soon you will be empowered." I knew my pride caused me to lose contact with Bob. I humbly confessed my error and was taken to the throne where I entered into worship.

I could hear the sound of rain. My thoughts turned to my spiritual family. Wisdom spoke, "You are done for now in this place. I leave you with this information. The timetable of Kingdom growth is in the hands of the family you were placed in along with other Kingdom families being raised up. Know there are others but keep your attention and devotion on your family. In the council of the righteous, there I will be with you. Keep the fire of urgency burning in you. Don't delay whenever possible."

Wisdom pointed and I saw that the realm of "come up here and I will show you" is open to those seeking first the Kingdom. I was shown many of the great and mighty things to come. I realized some had begun. I saw a company of Saints already living in this realm but they had yet to assemble on the earth. Their assembly was in the spirit as they were unconscious of their ascension, yet they were being prepared for specific locations of convergence on the earth. They were being prepared to enter the gateway through which you become conscious of the Kingdom realm on earth. I saw but a few and then suddenly, I saw multitudes without number. I thought to myself, "Could the catalyst to this multiplication be the vision I had earlier? The one I laid out in my first book on disciples?" I heard a voice say, "Present your case before the elders." I was confused as I didn't know if I should go to the Heavenly elders or human Church leadership of the Kingdom. A pause happened, followed by fighting in the heavenlies between the angels of God and those representing the kingdom of darkness.

I saw air leaving a balloon and knew it was darkness leaving the earth. I knew it was the Saints collapsing this darkness. I knew it was the Saints that found themselves, by the grace of God, in the "come up here and I will show you" realm. I knew they were Knowledge bearers—carriers of the knowledge of God-the information of the Kingdom. I could see they were dead, yet alive. I knew they were not yet in a resurrected state but dead enough to be used by the King. I could see them covered in a robe and on the robe read "RIGHTEOUSNESS—worthy is the Lamb." The words were pulsating like a heartbeat. I felt it was signaling to specific spirits of darkness, "Hands off. This Saint has not been perfected practically, but the imputed righteousness of Christ is understood."

Author's Note: I believe the carriers of the information of the Kingdom–the "knowledge bearers"–are soon to reappear on the earth. I see the mind of Elihu being formed in these future knowledge-bearers. These future sons of the Kingdom will soon echo the words of Elihu found in Job 36:2-4. *"Bear with me a little, and I will show you that there are yet words to speak on God's behalf. I will fetch my knowledge from afar ... for truly my words are not false; One who is perfect [whole] in knowledge is with you."*

The greatest obstacle to mankind is blindness to the Kingdom field of Consciousness. "Woe to you experts in the law, because you have taken away the key to knowledge. You yourselves have not entered, and you have hindered those who were entering." (Luke 11:52). This key is none other than information of the Kingdom taken in through the commitment to seek first the Kingdom. Stripping humanity of the information of the Kingdom by blinding us from understanding our need to make seeking the Kingdom our top priority, Satan has succeeded in removing the Kingdom's influence both in human consciousness and the earth. Ignorance is the kingdom of darkness' foundation. Everything Satan has built on earth came as a result of mankind's blindness to God's Kingdom. Once a man sees the Kingdom however, his life changes forever and the kingdom of darkness trembles. The Kingdom of Heaven is like yeast; what it enters it influences, eventually consuming everything. This all-consuming Kingdom chooses to begin its consumption of all things in the human heart. From there it moves out. If knowledge becomes the substance of the Kingdom, then the receiver of that knowledge becomes its container. All Kingdom containers are meant to release their substance, but not until they reach overflow. This requires time for the Kingdom within to grow and develop. Once its end is reached for a particular season, out of the abundance of the heart the mouth begins establishing Kingdom law. Kingdom Saints need to allow the cross to do deep work in all areas, especially on taming our tongue. It was said of Samuel that none of his words fell to the ground. He was a model for Kingdom communication.

> *"Not only so, but we ourselves, who have the first-fruits of the Spirit, groan inwardly as we wait eagerly for our adoption to sonship, the redemption of our bodies."*
>
> Romans 8:23

This word adoption in the Greek means the placing of a son as opposed to becoming a son. Because the seed of God was placed in you before the foundation of the world, your have been positioned in the family of God. My earthly father would never adopt me into his family because his seed is already in me. I am already a family member of the Gissibl name. Likewise is the case with our Heavenly Father.

When Paul uses the word adoption, he's not referring to adoption like we have been conditioned to think by our culture. We already are a son and daughter in God's family.

God adopts us by placing us in rulership because we are sons. This word adoption is more like the hiring of a family member that takes on an executive position in the family business rather than adoption of a child into a family. Adoption in the Kingdom is not a movement into a family but a movement within a family—from the responsibilities of a child into the responsibilities of an adult. If the Kingdom was a family business, then adoption would be promotion within the business. Adoption is an upgrade in responsibility and an increase in authority to grow the family business.

Not everyone will rule and reign with Christ. Only those who overcome will be entrusted with such honor.

"To him that overcometh will I grant to sit with me in my throne, even as I also overcame, and am set down with my Father in his throne."

Revelation 3:21 KJV

Responsibility in the family business has nothing to do with salvation but everything to do with your specific role and function in the Kingdom realm of consciousness, both now and for eternity. The overcomers are rising and will soon be placed in the family business, empowered to enact Kingdom business on earth as it is in Heaven.

Conclusion

We have entered a new season. This new season begins with an invitation to commit to a life of Jesus' highest priority—seeking the Kingdom. Accepting this invitation places you on a pathway that leads you through a gateway where entrance into the Kingdom realm of consciousness is realized. This new territory, the realm of the "come up here," is where Jesus is building His Church. It's the place where the mysteries of the Kingdom are revealed in your subjective experience, and you become clothed with the attributes of the Kingdom. It's the place where you become a living stone, joined together with others to build Kingdom consciousness on the earth. There is no greater endeavor than to lay down your life for the sake of the King and His Kingdom. There is no greater way to express laying down your life than to pick up Jesus' mandate to seek first the Kingdom. If not you then who and if not now then when?

One Final Thought

In Daniel chapter 4 Nebuchadnezzar has a dream. In it, he sees a tree that's the center of the earth. All living things are under its shadow as all of humanity is fed by it. The fruit of this tree is the life source of the entire human race. Nebuchadnezzar than sees a watcher angel come from Heaven and declare, in conjunction with a human carrying jurisdictional authority to speak for the Lord in the earth, *"Chop down the tree … This decision is by the decree of the watchers, and the sentence by the word of the holy ones, in order that the living may know that the Most High rules in the kingdom of men."* Nebuchadnezzar is then taken from man and placed in a field where he is fed a new diet, eaten in a specific manner, like a cow. Nebuchadnezzar then asks Daniel to interpret the dream, and this is his response (my paraphrase):

"My lord, may the dream concern those who hate you, and its interpretation concern your enemies!" Daniel continues by establishing the tree to be Nebuchadnezzar himself and declares, *"You will be driven from men, and your dwelling shall be with the living ones in a specific field. Here you will begin a new diet where you will receive new life through a new life source in the same manner in which a cow eats, digests, and assimilates grass. This process of receiving life will be covered with substance from Heaven, the dew of Heaven, so much so that a new experience of life will emerge out of a new life source. You shall know by experience that the Most High rules in the kingdom of men, and gives it to whomever He chooses."*

At this point, I want to transition from the dream and draw out some of its prophetic significance for our time, specifically for the rising overcomers. In order to do so, we must establish some of the typology and meaning within the dream. The following will establish such a task and in doing so will open understanding of its present-day significance.

In this dream, Nebuchadnezzar represents the carnal mind as it has become the life source of the kingdom of man on earth. All living creatures are in its shadow, and all of humanity is fed by it. The trees fruit is limited to the knowledge of good and evil which has imprisoned humanity in the field of carnal consciousness. Man's diet has been limited to substance drawn from the realm of consciousness of the carnal mind. The kingdom of man has been plugged into the kingdom of darkness, and its influence has reached its pinnacle. Daniel prayed, "may the dream concern those who hate you, and its interpretation concern your enemies!" The enemies of the carnal mind are those who have overcome its existence within and influence without. Those who hate the carnal mind are those who have entered the realm of the Kingdom on earth through the renewed mind.

We are entering a season where a group of Watcher angels will begin working with a group of Overcoming Saints to begin chopping down the tree of the carnal mind, damaging its ability to provide for humanity and ultimately eliminating the influence of the carnal mind. These "Watcher" angels, whose nature and intent is to awake ("Watcher" means to awaken), will find "holy one's" upon the earth. At the command of the Lord of Hosts, They will begin a season of declaration that will cause the life of the carnal mind to begin a process of death. Out of this death will emerge the Kingdom realm in man's consciousness—the life source of lasting Kingdom culture on earth. This inward transformation will make way for the outward transformation of the earth as the kingdom of man begins shifting back under the rulership of the Kingdom of light. The kingdom of man will begin a process of being taken out of the kingdom of darkness and lifted up into the Kingdom of light. As soon as the model of transportation is infused with Kingdom culture, multitudes will begin duplicating it. This will accelerate humanities lift into the Kingdom realm of consciousness. The rising "holy one's" will be the co-laborers with the Watcher angels that will be responsible for collapsing the carnal realm of consciousness while simultaneously making visible the Kingdom realm on earth.

I believe the "holy one's" that co-labor with the angels that awake are the overcomers found in Revelation 2:7. They are granted access to eat from the tree of life which grows the fruit responsible for bringing the experiential knowledge realized in the place where "the Most High rules in the kingdom of men." That place is the Kingdom realm of consciousness found by all who come out from under the realm of the carnal mind. When the Most High rules in the kingdom of men, the Kingdom of Heaven is once again established upon the earth as the field of consciousness through which humanity streams its experience. We are granted access to eat from the tree of life every time we seek the Kingdom. However, an accessional meal from the tree of life is not sufficient. Let not that man think he shall receive anything.

Partaking in a steady diet of the tree of life's fruit is the narrow way of the overcomer. An Overcomer must receive more nutrient's daily from the tree of life than from the tree of the knowledge of good and evil. The Overcomer is marked with the seed of seeking first the Kingdom. The difference between seeking the Kingdom and seeking FIRST the Kingdom is the difference between tasting the powers of the age to come and walking in the powers of the age to come. A buffet-style approach to seeking the Kingdom is to receive the heavenly gifts only to have them taken from you. To receive the entirety of your diet with seeking first the Kingdom nutrients is to enter the process of becoming the heavenly gifts.

Nebuchadnezzar, in the dream, sees himself entering a field and beginning a new diet. A specific diet eaten in a specific way. This new diet will "Let his heart [mind] be changed ... in order that the living may know that the Most High rules in the kingdom of men." This portion of the dream provides insight into the required method of receiving the nutrients necessary for enlightenment and ascension into the Kingdom realm. The dew that rests upon the grass represents added substance within the information of the Kingdom received while eating from the same field where the tree of life is rooted. It becomes necessary to eat this life source drenched with heavenly dew in a specific manner, like a cow. This analogy reflects the importance of chewing the information of the Kingdom over and over, allowing for the steady release of nutrient's (whole knowledge) from the new diet. Digesting and re-digesting; chewing and chewing again the whole knowledge (nutrients) grown in the field of the Kingdom. This is the process that connects us to the field of consciousness that enables us to "know" (experience) that the Most High rules in the kingdom of men on earth. This field, in the coming years, will be known as the field of Kingdomology.

Author's Note: The following provides deeper insight into the assimilating of nutrient's "like a cow." The biology of a cow is such that it has four stomachs and a unique digestive process to break down its food. When the cow eats, it first chews the food until it's able to be swallowed. The food travels to the first two stomachs where it is stored until later. When the cow is full from this phase of the eating process, it rests. Later, the cow coughs up bits of partially chewed food and begins chewing it again. This chewing culminates in a complete process, and the cow swallows it once again. The food then goes to the third and fourth stomachs where it becomes fully digested. Some of the digested food travels to the udder, where it is made into milk that will come out of her teats, while the rest goes towards the cow's nourishment. It's important for us to understand that there is more "nutrient's" than the initial revelation. Let this be an incentive for you to pick back up revelation in order to chew on it more, providing for further "whole knowledge" to come into you.

John the Baptist prophesied *"The ax is already at the root of the trees"* because Jesus, and likely John the Baptist, fulfilled the requirements necessary to co-labor with the Watcher angels to begin chopping down the outward tree of the carnal mind. The act of seeking first the Kingdom begins the process of chopping down Nebuchadnezzar's tree. To individually seek first the Kingdom is to begin chopping at the root of your individual carnal mind. A teacher whose carnal mind is chopped down and whose teaching the message of the Kingdom, is co-laboring with the Watcher angels to chop down Nebuchadnezzar's tree—the carnal mind that grows collective consciousness in and of the carnal realm.

We are in a season where a group of Watcher angels is being released to chop down the tree that's represented in Nebuchadnezzar's 2nd dream. The collapsing of the Romans 8:6-7 carnal mind has begun and will give rise to a pioneering group who will become "subject to the law of God" on earth, resulting in the establishing of Kingdom culture once again on earth. (*"Because the carnal mind is enmity against God; for it is not subject to the law of God, nor indeed can be ...."*)

The Watcher angels will be released in increased numbers as they see their partners—Overcomers subject to the law of God—come alive through the in sync action of the collapse of their carnal mind and the construction of their renewed mind. The earth, Heaven and those with eyes to see will witness the dawning of a strategic partnership between the Watchers and these Overcomers and their co-laboring efforts to chop down Nebuchadnezzar's tree. The chopping has begun and will continue as the Watchers decree it, and the judicial decision and mandate of the overcoming Saints declare it. Only those Saints who have overcome their carnal minds will be commissioned to co-labor with the Watcher angels for such an assignment. To overcome the carnal mind, you must seek first the Kingdom, whole knowledge, long enough to form the renewed mind.

To summarize, in Daniel 4, Nebuchadnezzar depicts a tree which represents the carnal mind. The tree that covered the earth is the carnal mind's influence over the earth. All of humanity has been eating the fruit of this tree as its appearance is deceivingly lovely (see Daniel 4:20-22). This tree, the carnal mind, has taken dominion of the entire earth (v22) but its pinnacle of influence has been reached. The kingdom built by the carnal mind is departing as "a voice came from heaven saying, *'This is what is decreed for you, King Nebuchadnezzar [the carnal mind]: 'Your royal authority has been taken from you'*" (v. 31). To the degree, the Saint's possessing the renewed mind arises is the degree the authority of the carnal mind is stripped. The kingdom of darkness, governed by the carnal mind, is falling.